AIRCRAFT

an all color story of modern flight

AIRCRAFT

an all color story of modern flight
David Mondey

Octopus
Octopus Books

First published 1973 by
Octopus Books Limited
59 Grosvenor Street, London W1

ISBN 0 7064 0271 5

© 1973 Octopus Books Limited

Distributed in USA by
Crescent Books
a division of Crown Publishers Inc
419 Park Avenue South
New York, N.Y. 10016

Distributed in Australia by
Rigby Limited
30 North Terrace, Kent Town
Adelaide, South Australia 5067

Produced by Mandarin Publishers Limited
14 Westlands Road, Quarry Bay, Hong Kong

Printed in Hong Kong

Contents

Note: Illustration figures which appear in **bold** type throughout the text refer to aircraft listed in the Tables of Technical Data at the end of the book.

Introduction

It was, of course, the birds who were responsible for the whole complicated business.

There was prehistoric man; two feet firmly on the ground; eking out a somewhat precarious living by hunting. There, too, was the bird; his two 'feet' sometimes firmly on the ground; pecking up a reasonable living from the land. When man attempted to add bird to his cookpot, bird spread wings and flew away.

The first encounters of this nature must have come as an eye-opener to man. The discovery of another two-legged creature winning a living from the land would have been a surprise. To learn that it could also fly in the air, over hill and dale, and consequently had a built-in means of travel and escape, would be a staggering revelation.

Thus began centuries of frustration for the pioneering types who felt that the human race must reach out to the sky. But as decade followed decade, it became clear that man could not fly; so, he endowed his gods with wings, as a symbol of their supernatural powers. Nevertheless, he still remained envious of the gods and the birds, who were able to cleave the canopy of the heavens on outstretched wings. Those who thought deeply about the problem concluded there was little likelihood that man might fly one day. It would be exciting, and useful, but it was really only a dream.

So matters remained until the sixteenth century was nearing its end, when a man with the brain of a scientist began to think seriously about attainment of the dream. This was Leonardo da Vinci (1452–1519), whose detailed study of bird flight nevertheless led him to the erroneous conclusion that man's muscular power, so superior to that of the birds, should enable him to fly in a properly constructed ornithopter, or flapping-wing aircraft.

The 'flappers' were legion. Since only the birds had been seen to fly it seemed reasonable to assume that, by copying their flapping-wing mode of locomotion, man might also succeed. In retrospect, one can only assume that their eyes were so tightly closed, to give animation to their dream, that they failed to notice the gulls, which soared majestically over their heads on slender, and often stationary, wings.

The death of da Vinci, in 1519, was the prelude to a period of more than a century which was virtually devoid of progress. When, in 1680, Giovanni Alphonso Borelli's *De motu animalium* was published posthumously, it was clear that, as a result of his detailed study of bird flight, man did not have the power output needed to lift himself and a machine into the air. Borelli's comment that: 'It is impossible that men should be able to fly craftily by their own strength', brought an end to practically all heavier-than-air experiments until the nineteenth century.

By the time they were resumed, man had already flown. True, this was in lighter-than-air craft, beginning with the 4 minute 24 second tethered flight made by Jean-Francois Pilâtre de Rozier in a Montgolfier hot-air balloon on 15 October 1783. Less than two months later a hydrogen-filled balloon had completed a successful two-hour free flight.

Man was inspired: at last he could enter the domain of the birds. There was, of course, a problem: it was a one-way journey, the direction of which was dictated by the caprice of the wind. Nonetheless, the balloon had its moment of glory and, in various roles, has survived into contemporary history. It served also another purpose: it captured the attention and imagination of a 10-year-old boy, George Cayley, who lived near Scarborough, Yorkshire.

Sir George Cayley (1773–1857) has been described in modern times as '. . . one of the most powerful geniuses in the history of aviation'. Such an honour was not bestowed without just cause: he was the first man to formulate the basic concept of mechanical flight, isolating the aerodynamic forces of lift, thrust and drag. In 1804 he built and flew the first really successful model aeroplane in history, a glider five feet in length. Five years later Cayley constructed a full-size glider with a wing area of 300 sq ft (27·87 m²), and by his 80th year had built a more-advanced man-carrying version. On this his reluctant coachman was carried over a small valley, in the grounds of Cayley's home at Brompton Hall.

From the time of that event, until the end of the nineteenth century, attempts at flight with heavier-than-air craft were dominated by the 'hoppers'. These were the pioneer builders, whose machines still lacked the compact, light-weight power plant needed to give birth to powered flight. As a result, however advanced their design, these aircraft could make only brief, uncontrolled hops, usually boosted into the air by starting their 'take-off' run down an inclined ramp.

But the time had arrived when the all-essential engine was only a few years away. Nineteen years after Cayley's death, Otto, in Germany, built a successful four-stroke engine that was powered by coal gas. Nine years later, Gottlieb Daimler adopted his fellow-countryman's four-stroke cycle to produce the world's first single-cylinder internal combustion engine. Twelve months later a Daimler engine was powering its first motor car.

This development of the internal combustion engine had no direct association with aviation. Serious experimenters, realizing that a great deal of time might be wasted if they just sat around and waited for someone to provide better engines than those being used by the 'hoppers', decided to use this interval to refine the design of the aeroplane's structure, or airframe.

Foremost among these men was the German, Otto Lilienthal (1848–1896), whose graceful and beautifully-constructed hang-gliders enabled him to become the first man in the world to fly confidently and regularly, amassing a total of rather more than 2,000 flights. He did not develop control surfaces for his gliders, but relied upon body movements to provide limited control in the three axes of pitch, roll and yaw.

Lilienthal recorded his progress in detail, tabulating the effects of variations in wing camber and aspect ratio, and it was his work that inspired Percy Pilcher in Britain (1866–1899) and Octave Chanute in America (1832–1910). But despite his methodic and unhurried approach, Lilienthal lost his life at the age of 48, on 10 August 1896, a day after one of his gliders stalled and crashed to the ground. Just over three years later, on 30 September 1899, Pilcher also crashed in his *Hawk* glider, and died from his injuries on 2 October. He, too, had relied upon body movement to provide some measure of control for his craft.

So, by 1900, Chanute was the only surviving member of this trio of early researchers. Four years earlier, thrilled by reports of Lilienthal's progress, he had designed several man-carrying gliders. He was then too old to pilot them himself, but secured the assistance of a young engineer to help with design and construction, as well as undertaking the job of 'test-pilot'.

Chanute's greatest contributions towards design refinement were the development of a biplane form of the Lilienthal-type glider, and the introduction of a new and successful form of biplane rigging. He made, also, a different kind of contribution towards powered flight by virtue of the fact that he lived in America and was able to communicate easily with the Wright brothers.

Wilbur (1867–1912) and Orville (1871–1948) Wright, bicycle-building sons of a minister, had been keenly interested in the possibility of mechanical flight from early years. Avidly reading the somewhat limited literature available, they acquired a copy of Chanute's *Progress in Flying Machines* and soon entered into correspondence with him. By 1900 they had become friends, and Chanute encouraged them in every possible way, providing information and discussing with them their early problems. In this manner, the experimental work of these three gliding pioneers directly assisted the Wrights to achieve their goal of powered flight.

Just a few weeks before Pilcher's death, the Wrights had completed their first biplane kite. By the Autumn of 1902 they had built their No. 3 glider. This was a practical machine that required only slight modification and a power plant to place the two brothers on the pedestal of immortality.

But, like all other would-be aviators, they still awaited the all-essential, lightweight power plant that was needed to thrust their aircraft through the air. The Wrights had thought this was one problem that would be resolved fairly easily for, by 1900, the motor car had already created a sensation in America. In 1902, for example, more than 2,000 Curved Dash 5 hp two-seat cars had been built by Oldsmobile.

Not surprisingly, the Wrights imagined that one of these many types of motor vehicle engine could be adapted fairly easily to power their aircraft. They were soon to discover that all of them were far too heavy, having regard to the very limited power they developed.

Typically, they decided to design and build their own. This emerged as a 12 hp four-cylinder water-cooled in-line engine, which had a gross weight (including fuel, water and accessories) of about 200 lb (91 kg), providing a weight to power ratio of 16·6 lb (7·53 kg)/hp. Even then it still needed a propeller, and there was precious little information to guide

them in its design. Once again they had to carry out their own research before it was possible to fashion the two pusher propellers needed for their *No. 1 Flyer*.

In this machine, at Kill Devil sands, near Kitty Hawk, North Carolina, on 3 December 1903, the dream became reality. The first 12-second 120 ft (36·6 m) flight was made by Orville, After some adjustments Wilbur took the controls for a second flight, as it was their practice to alternate as pilot. A total of four flights were made on that historic day, at the end of which Orville was able to telegraph to their father: 'Success four flights thursday morning all against twentyone mile wind started from level with engine power alone average speed through air thirtyone miles longest 57 seconds inform Press home Christmas.' The telegraphist had, in fact, made an error. It should have read 59 seconds. The distance covered was 852 ft (259·7 m).

This epoch-making event did not electrify the world: in fact the world knew virtually nothing about it until some years later. Instead, it was the efforts of a flamboyant little Brazilian living in France, Alberto Santos-Dumont, that scooped the world's headlines. During 1906, with his odd-looking No. 14-*bis* which was powered by a 50 hp Antoinette engine, he made a first flight of 197 ft (60 m) at Bagatelle, Paris, on 23 October. As newspapers carried the report of this event around the world, most people believed that Santos-Dumont really had made the first powered flight in history.

Just under three weeks later, on 12 November, Santos-Dumont again had No. 14-*bis* at Bagatelle. On that day he was to make an attempt to win a prize of 1,500 francs, offered by the Aéro Club de France, for the first aeroplane able to exceed a distance of 100 m (305 ft). Santos-Dumont and his aircraft 'rose' to the occasion, cheered by an enormous crowd that had flocked to the large open space at Bagatelle, in the Bois de Boulogne. They had come in anticipation of seeing an aero-

plane in flight for the first time, and they were not disappointed. As the crowd cheered itself hoarse, No. 14-*bis* excelled itself to record a flight of just over 21 seconds, covering a distance of 220 m (722 ft).

Among the spectators was Louis Blériot who, less than three years later, on 25 July 1909, was to demonstrate a rather frightening potential of the aeroplane by making the first successful flight across the English Channel. Even the most naïve militarist could appreciate that, as it developed, this vehicle would make nonsense of international boundaries: those in Britain realized that the broad moat of the Channel was no longer an assurance of insularity.

However, to Germany goes the accolade for being first to demonstrate what must be regarded as the most vital task of aviation, namely air transport. During the years 1910–1914 the Deutsche Luftschifffahrts A.G. Direktion, known universally as Delag, operated a fleet of four airships to provide a regular but unscheduled passenger service from Friedrichshafen. When the First World War brought this to an end, almost 170,000 miles (273,590 km) had been flown without serious accident, and more than 34,000 passengers had been able to sample the benefits of air travel.

One should remember that these lighter-than-air 'ships' gained their lifting capability from hydrogen gas: their engines were needed only to provide passage through the air and were not vital to keep them airborne. Heavier-than-air craft could not remain aloft for very long without the power of an engine or engines, and still lacked a really effective power plant.

Once again it was France that led the way, with a revolutionary new engine designed by Laurent Seguin. One of the

major problems of the period was that engines overheated, and either lost power or gave up the struggle. Seguin's idea was to fix the crankshaft and make the cylinders rotate, thus providing adequate cooling for them. The resulting engine, which became known as the rotary type, not only solved the problem of overheating, but the large rotating mass ensured smooth running.

Seguin's seven-cylinder Gnome engine of 1909 weighed 172 lb (78 kg) and developed 50 hp (3·4 lb : 1·54 kg/hp). This only six years after construction of the Wright engine. It represented the biggest single advance in the history of powered flight to that date, and the Gnome rotary dominated the aero-engine scene for several years.

So, at the beginning of the First World War, the aeroplane had begun to acquire a degree of reliability. Its range and payload were still very limited, but participation in pre-war army manoeuvres had demonstrated something of its potential as a weapon of war. Unfortunately, it held little appeal for the majority of military planners, who seemed to regard it as little more than an extremely expensive and

problematical pair of field glasses. It might prove to be an ideal reconnaissance vehicle; if it happened to be a fine day and the wind wasn't blowing too strongly.

In fact, it proved to be more than ideal for reconnaissance, and it was this particular class of machine that was the progenitor of the entire line of military aircraft. For as soon as it was appreciated how vital was the intelligence contribution made possible by this type of aeroplane, it became necessary to deny one's airspace to enemy machines. Thus, fighters were needed to shoot 'theirs' out of the sky; escorts were required to protect 'ours' sent on patrol; and eventually came the requirement for machines capable of attacking and destroying the bases from which 'their' aircraft operated.

By the war's end the lightweight aircraft which, at its beginning, had maintained a somewhat precarious hold on the insubstantial air, had given place to robust fighter aircraft like the British Sopwith Snipe, French SPAD XIII and German Fokker D.VIII. The last-named was, perhaps, the best all-round fighter type of that era, having a maximum speed of around 125 mph (201 km/h) and service ceiling of 21,000 ft (6,400 m).

To attack strategic targets in Germany, British designers and engineers had developed the long-range Handley Page V/1500. Completed too late to see service in the war, it was a four-engined giant that, carrying 7,500 lb (3,400 kg) of bombs, had a gross take-off weight of nearly 13½ tons and a range of 1,300 miles (2,092 km).

Germany had soon discovered that her Zeppelin airships were too vulnerable, when opposed by hostile weather and enemy aircraft, and had developed 'giants' of her own. The most impressive of these were the Zeppelin Staaken R series, the R.VI having four engines, four machine-guns, eighteen-wheel landing gear, and the capability of carrying eighteen 220 lb bombs internally. With a maximum take-off weight of just over 11¼ tons, it was used to make attacks on both France and Britain.

But despite this apparent progress, airframe construction had really made little advance. Improved aircraft resulted primarily from the gradual development of more reliable engines: engines with more than sufficient power to overcome the enormous drag of the unstreamlined and inefficient biplane structures, and which still had power in reserve.

In spite of such limitations, those concerned with the potential of civil aviation in the post-war world realized that it was no use waiting until the last shot had been fired before creating the necessary organization. Long before peace came, more astute businessmen began planning the civil airlines that would, one day, be expanded to provide international services around the world. In Britain, for example, there was no shortage of aeroplanes at the war's end. The Royal Air

Force had over 22,000, and the government was keen to sell surplus machines at bargain prices. Most of them were quite unsuitable for carrying passengers, but seemed capable of conversion. In any event they would have to suffice until something better came along.

The position was, of course, quite different in Germany. Under the restrictions imposed by Armistice negotiations she was forbidden to possess or construct military aircraft. This saw the rebirth of the glider as a sporting vehicle, and research aimed at increasing its efficiency paid out some valuable aerodynamic dividends. Yet, strangely enough, it was Germany that provided the first regular civil airline service. Using two-seat D.F.W.s and five-seat A.E.G. biplanes, Deutsche Luft Reederei inaugurated its 120-mile (193-km) Berlin-Weimar service on 5 February 1919.

It was not until just over six months later, on 25 August 1919, that George Stevenson-Reece became THE passenger on the world's first daily international air service, operated by the British company known as Air Transport & Travel Ltd. Crammed into the narrow rear fuselage of a de Havilland D.H.4A, occupying the space where the gunner had once stood, Stevenson-Reece shared the 'cabin' with an assortment of 'freight', and paid a single fare of £21 for the privilege. Comparing the value of £1 sterling at that time and now,

this sum would have been more than adequate in 1973 to carry him by air from Britain and across the Atlantic to America.

But even if the fare was expensive it was worthwhile: a man or woman who had travelled by air between London and Paris in 1919 was clearly of a special breed.

In fact, air transport was then at a stage when it was uncomfortable rather than unsafe. With thousands of keen-to-fly ex-military pilots on the market, the air service operators could afford to be choosy and select the best: so standards were high.

Admittedly, aircraft of the period were not too reliable: one of A.T. & T.'s held the inglorious record of twenty-two forced landings in a single flight between London and Paris. Fortunately, all were on dry land, and aircraft of that era could land so slowly that this presented no real hazard. In consequence, UK registered civil transport aircraft recorded less than one fatal accident per year in their first decade of operations.

So it was that ex-service pilots in military aircraft began to show the world that the aeroplane was very much more than a device for exterminating one's enemies.

It could carry travellers over international airways, bringing travel times far below those of more conventional forms of transport.

It could carry sacks of air mail successfully and profitably. Successfully, because sacks of mail didn't mind being kept waiting, half frozen or shaken about. Profitably, because

they could be squeezed and pummelled into odd corners to fill all available cargo space.

The aeroplane also provided ideal transport for the VIP cargoes—Valuable, Imperative and Perishable. Gold bullion or industrial diamonds were pretty safe from villains at umpteen thousand feet; medical supplies, urgent spares and newspapers helped make up the second category; and there was always a demand for things like cut flowers, lobsters and exotic fruits. Cargoes of this kind were among the earliest, and their volume has increased throughout the years.

It was also a combination of service or ex-service pilots and aircraft that began to blaze the air trails around the world. In 1919, Alcock and Brown, flying a converted Vickers Vimy twin-engined bomber, had cracked one of the hardest nuts. This was a west-east crossing of the North Atlantic, from St John's Newfoundland, to Clifden in Ireland (Eire), a non-stop flight taking 16 hrs 27 mins. Vimys were also used to achieve the first flights from England to Australia and South Africa.

Late in 1925 Alan Cobham made a survey flight to India

and Burma in a de Havilland D.H.50, completing 18,000 miles (28,968 km) in a flying time of 210 hrs. This confirmed that a service between England and these countries was feasible, and almost exactly a year later he made a similar survey of the route to South Africa. In June of 1926 he made a third survey flight to Australia and for this important work, which helped establish the British trunk air routes, he was knighted by King George V.

But the flight which really fired the enthusiasm of men and women around the world was the first west-east solo Atlantic flight. This was made by Charles Lindbergh, who took off from New York on 20 May 1927, flying the single-engined Ryan monoplane, *Spirit of St Louis*. He covered the 3,600 miles (5,794 km) between New York and Paris non-stop in 33 hrs 39 mins, receiving a hero's welcome in Europe and on his return to America. The impact of this achievement was enormous, creating a new worldwide interest in air travel. If one man in a single-engined aircraft could make a non-stop flight of over three and a half thousand miles, it was clear that aeroplanes were becoming pretty safe.

Twelve months later Captain Charles Kingsford Smith confirmed this when, with a crew of three, he triumphed over the vast expanse of the Pacific Ocean. Flying in a three-engined Fokker monoplane, appropriately named *Southern Cross*, they took off from San Francisco on 31 May and landed at Brisbane on 9 June, with intermediate stops at Honolulu and Suva. The 3,138 miles (5,211 km) that separated the Hawaiian and Fiji Islands represented the longest ocean crossing by air to that date.

Both of these ocean conquering flights had been made in monoplane aircraft, and it was at this period that the biplanes, whose multiplicity of struts and wires had helped create what Anthony Fokker described as 'built-in headwinds', were beginning to give way to clean-looking cantilever-wing monoplanes. Junkers and Platz had led the way in Germany, and their fellow-countryman, Adolph Rohrbach, had refined the construction of monoplane wings, introducing metal box-spars and smoothly-skinned metal surfaces.

Gradually, influenced by high-speed aircraft developed to compete in events such as the international Schneider Trophy races for seaplanes, and the Pulitzer trophy races in the US, monoplane aircraft began to oust the biplane in most spheres. There were some notable exceptions.

Geoffrey de Havilland designed a small two-seat biplane which he named the *Moth,* a machine that was primarily responsible for a worldwide expansion of private flying. It flew for the first time on 22 February 1925, proving to be an outstanding and extremely reliable aircraft, and was the type used by a young woman named Amy Johnson to fly from England to Australia in 1930. An improved version, the *Tiger Moth,* was a standard RAF trainer for 17 years, and large numbers of these machines are still being flown all over the world. They provide the kind of flying of which the pioneers had dreamed: simple, carefree and basic, with the slipstream on one's face. There is every reason to believe that many of them will still be airworthy on the 50th anniversary of the Moth's first flight.

And at a time when countries like Germany and America were using, or on the verge of introducing, monoplane civil airliners, Britain's Imperial Airways began to use the Handley Page H.P.42 on its European services, a 130 ft (39·6 km) span biplane, powered by four engines and able to carry 38 passengers. With their girder-braced biplane wings and massive fixed undercarriage they had a maximum cruising speed of about 100 mph (161 km/h), but offered standards of comfort and safety that no other transport of the period could equal. As a result, they carried more passengers between London and the Continent in the 1930s than did all other airliners combined, and without ever hurting a passenger until the last of them disappeared during a wartime flight in 1940.

But other ideas were developing in these early post-war years. In 1923, in Spain, Juan de la Cierva had made the first successful flight in his C.4 Autogiro, the progenitor of the helicopter. At first glance it seemed fairly conventional; then one realized that it had no wings, and that some madman had mounted the sails of a windmill horizontally above its fuselage.

In fact de la Cierva was far from mad. He was the first man to build a stable rotor, for earlier experimental rotary-wing aircraft had all suffered from a common tendency to roll over in flight. This happened because the rotor blade advancing into the airflow developed more lift than the opposing blade which was travelling in a contrary direction. The 'flapping-hinge' rotor developed by de la Cierva allowed the advancing blade to rise slightly, reducing its angle of attack and, consequently, its aerodynamic lift; the reverse process applied to the retreating blade and resulted in the first balanced rotor. This was to prove a major contribution towards the development of a single-rotor helicopter, but which did not materialize until 19 years later when, in America, Igor Sikorsky's VS-300 proved to be the world's first practical single-rotor helicopter.

In retrospect, the 1920s provided some of the most eventful years in the history of aviation. This is not really surprising, for aircraft designers and engineers around the world, like the alchemists of the middle ages, were all seeking an elixir that would generate a golden age of travel in the new dimension. It is to their undying credit that, in the main,

they succeeded.

Basic research in the science of aerodynamics was receiving new attention in many countries, as men began to appreciate that the provision of bigger and better engines was not the simple answer to their problems. Wing shapes and wing sections were investigated closely to find ways of increasing lift and reducing drag. Wing leading-edge slots had been designed by Frederick Handley Page (later Sir) in 1919, and this proved to be an invention that revolutionized safety factors at low flying speeds. Handley Page slots, as they have become known universally, ensure that the airstream flows smoothly over the upper surface of the wing, even at high angles of attack, postponing the critical loss of control when the wing becomes in a stalled condition. These slots were introduced on a wide scale towards the end of the 1920s. Another aerodynamic innovation of the period was the wing trailing-edge flap, which could increase the lift of the wing during take-off when set at a small angle, or offer lower, safer landing speeds when set at a maximum deflection. And as this research stressed the importance of streamlining, the first aircraft with retractable landing gear began to appear.

It was also a time when wood, fabric and wire began to give place to all-metal construction; when metal propellers gradually superseded those of wood; and when aero-engines began to acquire their own starting systems, slowly bringing to an end the hazardous practice of engine-starting by swinging the propeller by hand.

In any event, the time had come when many engines could not be started in this manner as, towards the end of the decade, power plants with an output exceeding 500 hp became generally available. There were, of course, far more powerful engines as, for example, the 1,900 hp Rolls-Royce 'R' that carried the Supermarine S.6 to victory in the 1929 Schneider Trophy Race.

In-line engines, however, suffered from cooling problems, and required a liquid coolant system. The additional weight of this, plus its potential vulnerability for combat aircraft, tended to offset the principal advantage of this type of engine: its small frontal area. This led to emphasis on development of the air-cooled radial, housed in low-drag cowlings, and its success was such that this type of engine was used to power the majority of the world's large transport aircraft, until eventually giving way to the gas turbine.

The possibility of using a gas turbine to power aircraft was also being studied in this period, and Dr A. A. Griffith conducted some early experiments on this type of power plant at the RAE at Farnborough.

Even more revolutionary were the early experiments made during this decade which, almost a half-century later, were to put men on the Moon. In America, Dr R. H. Goddard was pursuing a more or less independent programme of experimental rocketry. During the 1920s he began to study seriously how to use the high potential energy of liquid-propellants. And in Germany, Fritz von Opel used solid-propellant rockets to power a glider which, in 1928, attained a speed of 95 mph (153 km/h).

There was no shortage of ideas, and there were men of all nationalities who possessed, in abundance, the primeval urge to explore the new frontiers open to them now that man had broken free from the bonds that, for so long, had tied him to Mother Earth. In the pages that follow, the story of this great adventure is told in words and pictures, and it is fascinating to realize how accurately prognostic were the words of Lord Byron, penned in 1822: 'I suppose we shall soon travel by air-vessels; make air instead of sea-voyages: and at length find our way to the moon, in spite of the want of atmosphere.'

Trainers and Light Craft

In a class of its own was the *Moth,* designed by Geoffrey de Havilland, and which flew for the first time on 22 February 1925. Strong, safe, easy to fly, it initiated the flying club movement around the world, making it possible for ordinary men and women to fly like the birds. Cheap to buy and cheap to operate, being powered by an engine of only 65 hp, it even had easily-folded wings so that it could be kept in a garage.

From it evolved the *Tiger Moth* (**1** below), a two-seat trainer, which flew for the first time on 26 October 1931. It entered service with the RAF in February 1932, and was finally retired from the RAF Volunteer Reserve in 1951, thus being the last biplane trainer used by the service. Over 1,000 had been delivered by the time the Second World War started, during which a further 4,005 were built for the RAF. To satisfy the needs of the Commonwealth Air Training Plan, a total of 2,949 were built by manufacturers in Australia, Canada and New Zealand.

Homebuilt aircraft have been with us since the first days of powered flight for, after all, the pioneer aviators began the homebuilding movement. It was not until after the Second World War that its activity began to assume large-scale proportions, particularly in America. Many of them are one-offs, designed and built by enthusiasts with special knowledge of aircraft design. Conversely, some are so successful that their designers make plans, and sometimes kits of parts, available to other amateur constructors.

In Britain the Popular Flying Association (PFA) looks after the interests of homebuilders, and some notable aircraft have been designed by its members. One of these is the *Taylor Monoplane* (**2** opposite top left), designed by the late Mr John Taylor, which has been and is being built by amateur constructors around the world. The example illustrated, with retractable landing gear, was built in the US by Mr Robert Ladd.

America's equivalent to the PFA is the Experimental Aircraft Association (EAA), which in 1971 had 68,000 members who had built more than 4,000 aircraft and had over 12,000 under construction. As a service to its members the EAA designed a single-seat sporting biplane and this, the *EAA Biplane* (**3** opposite top right), flew for the first time on 10 June 1960.

The standards of construction and finish are often very high, rivalling that of professional manufacturers, and awards offered by the EAA at their annual 'fly-ins' help to maintain these desirable characteristics. Designs, too, though slanted to make the task of building as simple as possible for the unskilled amateur, often provide quite professional-looking aircraft. Typical is the high-wing monoplane designed by James Bede and designated *BD-4* (**4** opposite below), of which well over 500 were under construction in 1972.

Other designers have approached the problem in a quite different manner, sacrificing appearance for extreme simplicity of construction, but in so doing have not overlooked structural integrity. One that is safe, easy to fly and maintain, is the *Aerosport Rail* (**5** left) designed by Mr H. L. Woods. Powered by an economical 33 hp two-stroke engine, the Rail has a top speed of 95 mph (153 km/h).

And more than one aircraft which originated as a homebuilt project has, because of its rugged structure and flight characteristics, progressed far beyond the homebuilt category. A good example is the *PL-1 Laminar* (**6** above), designed by Ladislao Pazmany. In 1968 a set of drawings were acquired by the Aeronautical Research Laboratory of the Chinese Nationalist Air Force in Taiwan. Following construction and testing of a prototype it was decided to adopt the type as a basic trainer, and 40 aircraft designated PL-1B have been built for the CAF and 10 for the Nationalist Chinese Army. A slightly modified version, the PL-2, may have even

more success. The Vietnam, Royal Thai and Korea Air Forces have each built a prototype. So, also, has the Miyauchi Manufacturing Company in Tokyo, which hopes to market this remarkable 'homebuilt' as a production aircraft.

Private flying has grown to enormous proportions in the US, comprising not only the homebuilders, but a much larger number of enthusiasts who do not have the time, or sufficient confidence, to join the do-it-yourself constructors.

They are well catered for by manufacturers like Cessna Aircraft Company at Wichita, Kansas, who in 1972 became the first company to complete its 100,000th aircraft. Their principal sales come from two/four-seat lightplanes, but not all of these go to private individuals. The *Cessna floatplane* (**7** below) illustrated would have delighted the hearts of the pioneers, for this is how they believed the aeroplane should be used: for recreation. Here, on Lake Mavora, New Zealand, it has carried a small party to fish in idyllic setting.

Under the collective heading of 'general aviation' is included not only private aircraft, used 'just for fun', but also business and executive machines. The smaller business aircraft are often in the four/six-seat category, powered by two engines, and the *Cessna 310* (**8** top) is a good example, of which well over 3,000 had been marketed by 1972. With a wingspan of only 36 ft 11 in (11·24 m), and two 260 hp engines, the Model 310 can fly safely on only one engine, and has a maximum range of about 1,700 miles (2,735 km).

In America, large-scale manufacture of lightplanes is not confined to Cessna. Two other constructors, Beech Aircraft Corporation and Piper Aircraft Corporation, make up a trio of manufacturers often called 'the big three'.

Beechcraft was founded in 1932, and one of its early successful aircraft was the *Model H18* (**9** above). A twin-engine light transport, with accommodation for a pilot, co-pilot and seven to nine passengers, its two 450 hp radial air-cooled engines give it a maximum level speed at 4,500 ft (1,370 m) of 236 mph (380 km/h). Its success may be measured by the fact that when production ended in 1969 a total of 9,388 of the Model 18 series had been built. More than 32 years had elapsed since the first flight of a Model 18, on 15 January 1937, representing the longest continuous production record of any aircraft.

Quantity-wise, this record may well be beaten by Beechcraft's 'butterfly'-tailed Model V35B *Bonanza* (**10** right), a graceful four/six-seat light cabin monoplane of which 9,288 had been built at the beginning of 1972. Powered by a single 285 hp engine, it has a maximum level speed of 210 mph (338 km/h) and a range in excess of 1,000 miles (1,609 km).

No less famous are the lightcraft produced by Piper Aircraft Corporation, at Lock Haven, Pennsylvania. Typical of their earlier products is the four-seat *Tri-Pacer* (**11** above right), seen cruising serenely above the clouds.

Like America but on a somewhat smaller scale, Europe has a thriving lightplane industry.

Typical of French products in this field is the four/five-seat DR 253 Régent (**12** above), built by Avions Pierre Robin. Known originally as Centre Est Aéronautique, this company produces some 150 lightplanes each year. The Régent is of wooden construction, and was the first Robin type to switch from tailwheel to tricycle landing gear in 1967.

In Britain the light aircraft industry has never had the same potential as in the US, for indifferent weather, high fuel costs and lack of air space, among other things, have been a barrier to real progress. In consequence, few companies have enjoyed the success that was merited by the designs they produced. Perhaps typical were the Auster and Miles companies, eventually taken over by Beagle Aircraft Ltd, a company that was itself acquired by the British Government in 1968 to ensure continuation of light aircraft development.

Even this move failed to provide security for Beagle and, two years later, the company went into voluntary liquidation. It had, nevertheless, produced some excellent lightcraft and examples of the B.121 *Pup,* a two/three-seat cabin monoplane and B.206 five/eight-seat twin-engine light executive are shown in the illustration (**13** above left).

Air races with small, fast aircraft have long been a feature of the American general aviation scene, and form an activity that has a large following. A US airline pilot, Captain Tom Cassutt, designed and built in 1954 a single-seat racing monoplane known as the Cassutt Special. The type had considerable success and many have since been built by homebuilders.

As part of a scheme to introduce this kind of air racing in Britain, Airmark Ltd built in 1969 their first Airmark/Cassutt 111M (**14** below left). Powered by a 95 hp Rolls-Royce/Continental engine it has a maximum level speed of 196 mph (315 km/h).

The American homebuilder has not been limited to fixed-wing aircraft. Typical of many small rotary-wing aircraft is the Bensen B-8M *Gyro-Copter* (**15** centre right), designed for home construction from kits or plans.

No mere toy, Mr Igor Bensen's B-8M captured a series of international records in 1967, including an altitude of 7,275 ft (2,717 m) and a speed of 79 mph (127·15 km/h) over a 15 km course.

Attempts have been made in America to attract the private pilot with rather more sophisticated light autogyros.

Umbaugh Aircraft developed between 1957–62 a two-seat light autogyro known as the Model 18-A. Air & Space Manufacturing built over 100 examples of a slightly modified version. In 1972 Farrington Aircraft Corporation acquired manufacturing rights, and the aircraft illustrated (**16** below right) is a proposed Forward Air Control version, with provision for air-to-ground rockets for target marking.

Reconnaissance

The reconnaissance role of the aeroplane, quickly proven to be vital soon after the beginning of the First World War, has continued to grow in importance.

Following the Second World War, at the end of which America had twice demonstrated operationally the awesome power of the atomic bomb, it was hoped that a new era of peace would bring relief to a shaken world. It was a vain hope, and an impasse dubbed the 'cold war' developed between East and West. When Russia detonated its first atomic bomb in 1949, peace through fear became the rule of the day.

In July 1955, at a Summit Conference in Geneva, American President Dwight D. Eisenhower proposed an 'Open Skies' policy, one of mutual photographic reconnaissance between East and West. The moment was too soon: the Soviet nation was not then ready to disclose to anyone her build-up of nuclear power.

At this time, in America, the brilliant aircraft designer 'Kelly' Johnson, of the Lockheed Company, proposed a revolutionary reconnaissance aircraft that would fly so high there was little chance of it being intercepted, and which would have sufficient range to overfly the vast territory of the Soviet Union.

This was the famous Lockheed U-2 (**17** below), with a camera that could spot golf balls on a putting green from 55,000 ft (16,800 m). It is best remembered for the Gary Powers incident, when this pilot in his U-2 was shot down over Russia by an anti-aircraft missile. It should be honoured for the fact that this type of unarmed reconnaissance aircraft

first alerted the world to the presence of Russian-built missiles on Cuba, late in 1962, so enabling the United States to prevent the development of a situation that could have initiated a Third World War.

Aircraft like the Lockheed U-2 satisfy a strategic reconnaissance role. When it is necessary to take a low-level close look at an enemy's forces, tactical reconnaissance aircraft are needed.

Typical is the American-built McDonnell Douglas RF-4E Phantom II (**18** right), a Mach 2 plus aircraft in service with the Federal German *Luftwaffe*. In addition to conventional cameras, it is equipped with electronic sensors, including infra-red detectors that can locate heat sources such as the exhaust gases of tanks and transport vehicles.

Probably the fastest and hottest reconnaissance aircraft in the world is Lockheed's SR-71A (**19** below right)—the SR standing for strategic reconnaissance—another brainchild of 'Kelly' Johnson.

So secret that performance figures have never been released, it is reported to be capable of sustained flight at Mach 3, have a ceiling of approximately 80,000 ft (24,385 m) and range of nearly 3,000 miles (24,385 km).

Perhaps the greatest problem in the design of this amazing aircraft was to provide a structure that could survive kinetic heating, caused by air friction, which raises its average over-all temperature to some 500–600 degrees F (260–316 degrees C).

The first illustration (**21** below left) shows a Douglas DC-130A 'mother plane' carrying two Ryan Model 154 RPVs. The second (**22** below) lets us see the beginning of a typical mission. In the setting sun a 'mother' climbs away with a single Model 147 RPV: nearer the target area she will launch, control and recover her wide-eyed 'baby' when its reconnaissance mission is completed.

The maintenance of peace by fear of nuclear annihilation has been with us for a long time. During these years, both East and West have sought to gain a telling advantage. When America first intro-

To keep a close watch on the Vietcong, American forces needed a new kind of reconnaissance aircraft: one that could cruise silently just above the tree-tops.

Lockheed produced two prototypes of a strange-looking craft: a combination of a sailplane, with a well-silenced engine, and a large-diameter multi-blade slow-turning propeller. It worked, and proved capable of flight as low as 100 ft (30 m) above hostile forces without being detected.

From these first Q-Star prototypes has been developed the more sophisticated YO-3A (**20** top), which carries electronic sensors that can detect an enemy under the most adverse conditions.

Rocketing in low over enemy-held territory on a reconnaissance sortie is no

enviable task. Inevitably, irreplaceable pilots and valuable aircraft are lost. Machines can be replaced; but lives are precious.

Back in the mid-thirties, radio-controlled versions of *Tiger Moths*, known as *Queen Bees*, had been used to provide targets for anti-aircraft gunners. And heaven help the poor individual that destroyed one!

It was soon appreciated that similar aircraft, with remotely-controlled cameras, would make an ideal reconnaissance vehicle. From such humble beginnings have developed companies like Teledyne Ryan Aeronautical in America, constructors of a whole family of drones and remotely-piloted vehicles. The former usually operate to a pre-set programme; the latter are flown by human pilots clear of the target area.

duced nuclear-powered submarines that could launch long-range ballistic missiles from beneath the sea, it was thought that this was the ultimate weapon. It was not long before the Soviet Union had a similar capability.

Thus, maritime reconnaissance has assumed a new importance, and the latest addition to Britain's armoury is the Hawker Siddeley *Nimrod* MR.Mk.1 (**23** right). Derived from the civil *Comet* 4C, it first entered service late in 1969. Capable of a 12-hour oceanic search, it carries equipment to detect and weapons to destroy the submarine hidden in the ocean's depths.

Fighters

At a time when civil transport aircraft were turning to monoplane construction, military aircraft—especially in Britain—were largely of biplane configuration. It is surprising, in retrospect, that the lessons learned from the Schneider Trophy Contests took so long to sink in. When the Second World War began in 1939, several RAF squadrons were still equipped with a biplane fighter.

It was, of course, an exceptional machine; the culmination of all that was best in biplane construction, providing a fast (253 mph: 407 km/h), highly-manoeuvrable aircraft armed with four Browning machine-guns. Last biplane fighter of the RAF, the Gloster *Gladiator* (**24** below) has nostalgic and historic associations that time will never tarnish.

Biplane fighters like the *Gladiator,* and its predecessor the *Gauntlet,* soon disappeared from front-line service when the RAF began to receive its first eight-gun monoplane fighters: the Hawker *Hurricane* (**25** below right) and Supermarine *Spitfire* (**26** right).

The names of these two aircraft, closely linked with the Battle of Britain, were known—and will always be remembered—by men and women with little or no knowledge of aviation history. But the same people might be surprised to learn that the *Hurricane,* the RAF's first fighter capable of a speed in excess of 300 mph (483 km/h), destroyed more enemy aircraft during the Battle of Britain than did all other defences, air and ground combined.

Designed by R. J. Mitchell who is also remembered for his superb S.6B racing seaplane which won the Schneider Trophy outright for Britain in 1931, the *Spitfire* was remarkable for its amazing development potential. The eight-gun *Spitfire* 1A in service at the beginning of the war had a maximum speed of 355 mph (571 km/h) at 19,000 ft (5,790 m). The Griffon-engined *Spitfire* XIV in service at the war's end, which destroyed an impressive number of V-1 flying-bombs, could attain a speed of 448 mph (721 km/h) at 26,000 ft (7,925 m).

When Britain declared war on Germany, on 3 September 1939, its first-line Fleet Air Arm squadrons were equipped, in the main, with a somewhat antiquated-looking biplane known as the Fairey *Swordfish* (**27** above).

Despite its appearance, it remained on operational service in the European theatre throughout the Second World War and, nicknamed the 'Stringbag', gained imperishable fame that rivals that of the *Spitfire*.

The *Swordfish*, torpedo-bombers extraordinary, first made famous during the Norwegian campaign, were involved in the hunting and destruction of the *Bismarck*; figured in the heroic but fruitless attacks on the German battleships *Scharnhorst, Gneisenau* and *Prinz Eugen,* while these vessels were making their historic Channel dash in February 1942; and recorded their greatest achievement with the destruction of the Italian fleet in Taranto harbour on the night of 11 November 1940.

De Havilland's 'wooden wonder', the elegant twin-engined *Mosquito* (**28** below), was built in bomber, fighter and reconnaissance versions.

The original concept was for a bomber that would carry no armament, relying upon speed to avoid interception by the enemy. Coupled with revolutionary wooden construction, this was sufficient to suggest it was something of a freak and government officials were highly sceptical.

When the prototype made its first demonstration flight the same officials were amazed when it flashed low over their heads at nearly 400 mph (644 km/h), and could hardly believe their eyes when it performed a series of upward rolls—on the power of only one engine.

The prototype of the most widely used of the Mosquito fighters (HJ 662) made its first flight in February 1943, and more than 2,500 of this Mk VI version were built eventually. With two 1,710 hp Rolls-Royce Merlin XXX engines, it had a maximum level speed of 407 mph (655 km/h) at 28,000 ft (8,535 m).

First jet fighter to enter service with the RAF, the Gloster *Meteor* (**29** above right) was also the first jet fighter to be used on operational service in the world, and the only Allied jet aircraft to be used in action during the Second World War.

First flown on 5 March 1943, it was not until well over a year later, on 12 July 1944, that the first two operational aircraft were delivered to No 616 Squadron.

On 7 September 1946, flown by Group Captain E. M. Donaldson, a *Meteor* F.4 raised the world speed record to 616 mph (991 km/h).

When Gloster *Meteor* jet fighters were first entering operational service in 1944, Supermarine's drawing office was busy with the designs for a similar category of aircraft. When this machine, named *Attacker,* entered service seven years later, it became the Royal Navy's first operational jet fighter.

This was superseded from March 1953 by the Hawker *Sea Hawk,* a clean-looking aircraft that stemmed from Hawker's first jet fighter, the P.1040. Used operationally from the carriers *Albion, Bulwark* and *Eagle* in 1956, in support of Anglo-French landings in Egypt, the type remained in service until 1960.

Illustrated is a *Sea Hawk* (**30** below right) serving with the German Navy.

In 1946 the Royal Air Force began to receive its first de Havilland *Vampires*.

It was no easy matter to train pilots to fly these new and somewhat breathtaking aircraft. Not only were they very fast, by comparison with piston-engined fighters, but their take-off and landing techniques were very different.

For basic training, the veteran *Tiger Moth* had been replaced at first by the Hunting Percival *Provost*. With this more powerful trainer the RAF initiated what became known as the *Provost/Vampire* training sequence.

When a somewhat revised *Jet Provost* (**31** above) became available, RAF Flying Training Command began an ex-

periment, in August 1955, to see whether piston-engined or jet-engined basic trainers were the best approach to flying turbine-powered fighter aircraft. In the competitive experiment which followed it soon became clear that the *Jet Provost* was best, and the type became the RAF's first turbine-powered basic trainer.

Canada, too, elected to use jet-powered trainers, thus ensuring that novice pilots of the Royal Canadian Air Force became conversant with turbine power plants from their first moment in the air. Canadair CT-114 *Tutors* (**32** top), the first of which had been built as a private venture, were ordered into production for the RCAF in 1961.

In post-war years, British aircraft manufacturers have suffered innumerable frustrations imposed by successive governments. Consequently, development of highly-advanced air-superiority fighters, such as the American F-14 and F-15 has not taken place.

Most successful of the post-war jet fighters have been the subsonic Hawker *Hunter* (**33** above right), still in service with the air forces around the world, and the BAC (formerly English Electric) *Lightning* (**34** right). First supersonic fighter designed for the RAF, the *Lightning*, which has a speed of over Mach 2, first entered service with No 74 Squadron in 1960.

The Royal Navy's first single-seat fighter capable of supersonic flight was the swept-wing Supermarine *Scimitar*, a machine which introduced a number of innovations, including advanced aerodynamic features to reduce take-off and approach speeds, and a power-operated control system. The type first entered operational service in June 1958, gradually superseding the *Sea Hawk*. The illustration (**35** top) shows *Scimitars*, wings folded, on the runway at Farnborough.

To meet an Admiralty requirement for a carrier-borne aircraft capable of delivering a nuclear weapon by low-level attack, sneaking in below enemy radar defences, Blackburn developed their *Buccaneer* S.1 (**36** above), and this entered operational service with the Royal Navy in July 1962.

Able to carry an 8,000 lb (3,628 kg) load of conventional

or nuclear weapons, distributed between internal stowage and underwing pylons, it was superseded by the more powerful Spey-engined *Buccaneer* S.2 in October 1965. A production S.2 was the first FAA aircraft to make an unrefuelled non-stop Atlantic crossing on 4 October 1965, completing the 1,950 miles (3,138 km) between Goose Bay, Labrador, and Lossiemouth, Scotland, in 4 hrs 16 mins.

America, too, had retained its share of biplane military aircraft during the between-wars period.

However, during 1931 the Boeing Company and the USAAC evolved jointly the design of a stubby-looking wire-braced low-wing monoplane that began to enter service on 16 December 1933 under the designation P-26A (**37** overleaf).

In addition to being the first monoplane fighter of the

USAAC, it was also the first all-metal fighter to enter production, and remained in service with front-line squadrons until shortly before the United States became involved in the Second World War.

Already in mass production before the Second World War began, the Lockheed P-38 *Lightning* (**38** top) was a highly successful aircraft, remaining in service with the USAAC (subsequently the USAAF), throughout the war.

When the *Lightning* began to join front-line squadrons, its gross weight exceeded that of some contemporary bombers. Nevertheless, it could attain a speed of 390 mph (628 km/h) at 20,000 ft (6,100 m).

The *Lightning* was responsible for a remarkable operation in the Pacific theatre when, after US intelligence had de-coded a secret Japanese signal, P-38Gs of the 339th Fighter Squadron intercepted and destroyed a transport aircraft carrying Admiral Yamamoto.

The first jet aircraft adopted by the USAAF for operational service was the Lockheed P-80. It was followed by the Republic F-84 *Thunderjet* (**39** above), which was the last subsonic straight-wing fighter-bomber used on operations, proving particularly valuable in the Korean War.

It has another distinction so far as the USAF is concerned, being the aircraft with which flight-refuelling techniques for fighters were developed.

Large numbers of *Thunderjets* were built for NATO forces, the example illustrated being an F-84F in service with the Norwegian Air Force.

Basic training satisfactorily ended does not mean that the new pilot can step straight into the cockpit of a high-performance and costly single-seat jet fighter and streak off into the 'wild blue'. As in Britain, America has also had to develop trainer versions of these more potent aircraft.

In December 1945 the USAAF began to receive its first jet fighter, the Lockheed P-80 *Shooting Star*, and it soon became clear that a trainer version was essential. This, the T-33 (**40** above), was produced by lengthening the fuselage of the standard P-80, to provide room for a second cockpit in tandem, and the bubble canopy was extended to cover both cockpits.

The type eventually became the USAF's standard jet trainer, many being supplied to foreign nations under the Military Aid Program, and a total of nearly 6,000 were built.

During the war, German scientists had discovered that the build-up of shock waves on the leading-edge of the wing

could be postponed by sweeping it aftwards, so that the angle formed by wing leading-edge and fuselage was less than 90 degrees.

In America, a new jet fighter had been designed for the USAF, but when details of the German research became available it was decided to change the design to incorporate this feature. Thus, North American's F-86 *Sabre* (**41** above right) became the USAF's first swept-wing fighter.

Lockheed's F-104 *Starfighter* (**42** right) was the world's first operational fighter aircraft capable of sustained flight at speeds in excess of Mach 2.

Tailored neatly around a powerful turbojet engine, its elongated fuselage and short-span wings made it look more like missile than aircraft. Not surprisingly, it needed a long take-off run, and the illustration shows a *Luftwaffe* F-104G involved in a zero-length launch test, being hurtled into the air by a large booster rocket.

It was fortunate that Ling-Temco-Vought's F-8 *Crusader* (**43** top) did not need a similar take-off run to Lockheed's *Starfighter,* being an air-superiority fighter designed for operation from the US Navy's aircraft carriers.

The first production aircraft went to the Navy's VF-32 Squadron in March 1957, but the F-8Es illustrated, aboard the carrier USS *Independence,* did not enter service until September 1961. Equipped with search and fire-control radar, the *Crusaders* can carry air-to-air or air-to-surface missiles, bombs and rockets.

When, in 1963, the US Navy initiated a design com-

petition for a light attack aircraft, Ling-Temco-Vought proposed a machine based on the F-8 *Crusader.*

Designated A-7 *Corsair* II, LTV's new Navy attack aircraft, which first entered service with training squadrons in 1966, is a subsonic machine which can carry up to 20,000 lb (9,072 kg) of offensive weapons.

Illustrations show A-7As of Squadron VA-147, lined up aboard a carrier, with wings-folded (**44** above); an A-7A with *Snakeye* bombs on an overland night patrol (**45** right); and a thirsty A-7D taking on fuel from a KC-135 tanker (**46** above right) before going in to attack.

Modern aerodynamicists have to try and answer '64-Dollar' questions like: 'Is a swept-wing or a straight-wing best for our new Superfast fighter?' The answer is not easy for, in general, the former is better for high-speed flight; the latter for slower speeds, and especially during take-off and landing.

Designers eventually tried to provide the best of both worlds in the variable-geometry wing, more commonly known as the 'swing-wing', and General Dynamics Corporation introduced this feature in the F-111 which was designed for service with both the USAF and USN. In the event, it became operational only with the former.

Illustrations show the wings in the fully-forward position (**47** above), as for take-off and landing, and fully-swept (**48** left) for high-speed flight.

In mid-1968 the US Navy requested five American aerospace companies to prepare designs for a new air-superiority fighter for the Navy. Grumman were winners of this design competition, and the resulting F-14A *Tomcat* (**49** far right) prototype made its first flight on 21 December 1970.

To gain a significant performance advance over the F-4 *Phantom II* currently in service, the *Tomcat* has powerful turbofan engines and unique configuration, including variable-geometry wings.

It is required to fulfil three primary

missions. The first of these, fighter sweep/escort, involves clearing contested airspace of enemy fighters, as well as protecting the strike force. Its second role will be to defend carrier task forces, and the third to attack ground tactical targets. It was scheduled to enter service with the fleet in 1973.

Fighter of the future, so far as the USAF is concerned, is the McDonnell Douglas F-15A *Eagle* (**50** above), photographed during the first flight of the prototype on 27 July 1972.

Its Pratt & Whitney advanced technology turbofan engines are so powerful that their thrust exceeds the weight of the *Eagle,* which is scheduled to enter service with the USAF in 1974.

The Northrop F-5E *Tiger II* single-seat twin-jet tactical fighter aircraft (**51** centre right) is intended primarily to provide America's allies in Southeast Asia with air-to-air superiority over the most advanced aircraft likely to be deployed against them.

Successor to the Northrop F-5, of which more than 1,150 are being supplied to American allies under the Military Assistance Program, the *Tiger II* will rely upon manoeuvrability rather than speed, and has special aerodynamic features to provide such characteristics.

Initial deliveries of 10 training aircraft will go to the USAF before deliveries to foreign governments begin.

After the Second World War seaplanes and flying-boats soon began to disappear from the aviation scene.

The long-range aircraft developed during the war offered great reliability, and the aerodynamic efficiency of a well-streamlined landplane was superior to that of a flying-boat of equivalent payload.

Gradually, flying-boats were supplanted for the duty of maritime patrol, being replaced by specially-designed aircraft like the Lockheed P-2 *Neptune*. More than a thousand of these fine aircraft were built for the US Navy and other services, and the P-2H *Neptune* (**52** right) illustrated was a variant used by the Maritime Patrol Command of the Canadian Armed Forces.

A small number of P2V-2 and P2V-7 *Neptunes* (**53** above) are in service with ski landing gear for operations in the Antarctic.

The land-based Neptune, once viewed rather sceptically by the US Navy, had proved so successful that in 1957 they sought a replacement. To save time in getting the aircraft into service it was suggested that a variant of a type then in production would be most suitable for this requirement.

So developed Lockheed's Model 186, which retained the wings, tail unit, power plant and other components of the commercial Electra, as well as much of the fuselage structure which was, however, shortened and provided with a weapons bay.

The first of the new anti-submarine aircraft went to operational units in 1961 under the designation P-3A *Orion*. The later P-3C *Orion* (**54** above right) illustrated carried an A-NEW data processing system, in addition to the advanced electronics, search stores and impressive weapons load of the earlier versions.

Perhaps better than anything else this illustration (**55** right) creates the atmosphere of the endless watch for submarines.

Engaged in an exercise, a US Navy submarine surfaces following its detection by a two-engined *Neptune* and a four-engined *Orion* ASW aircraft.

Most sophisticated of the US Navy's submarine hunter/killers is the Lockheed S-3A *Viking* (**56** above), which is scheduled to enter service some time early in 1974.

Control of the aircraft during long patrols is maintained by a computer-directed automatic flight-control system, leaving the crew of four free to concentrate on the 'needle-in-a-haystack' task of finding a hostile submarine.

The *Viking* carries the most advanced electronic equipment to simplify its hunter role, and an armoury of lethal weapons to ensure a certain kill of the very dangerous undersea weapon.

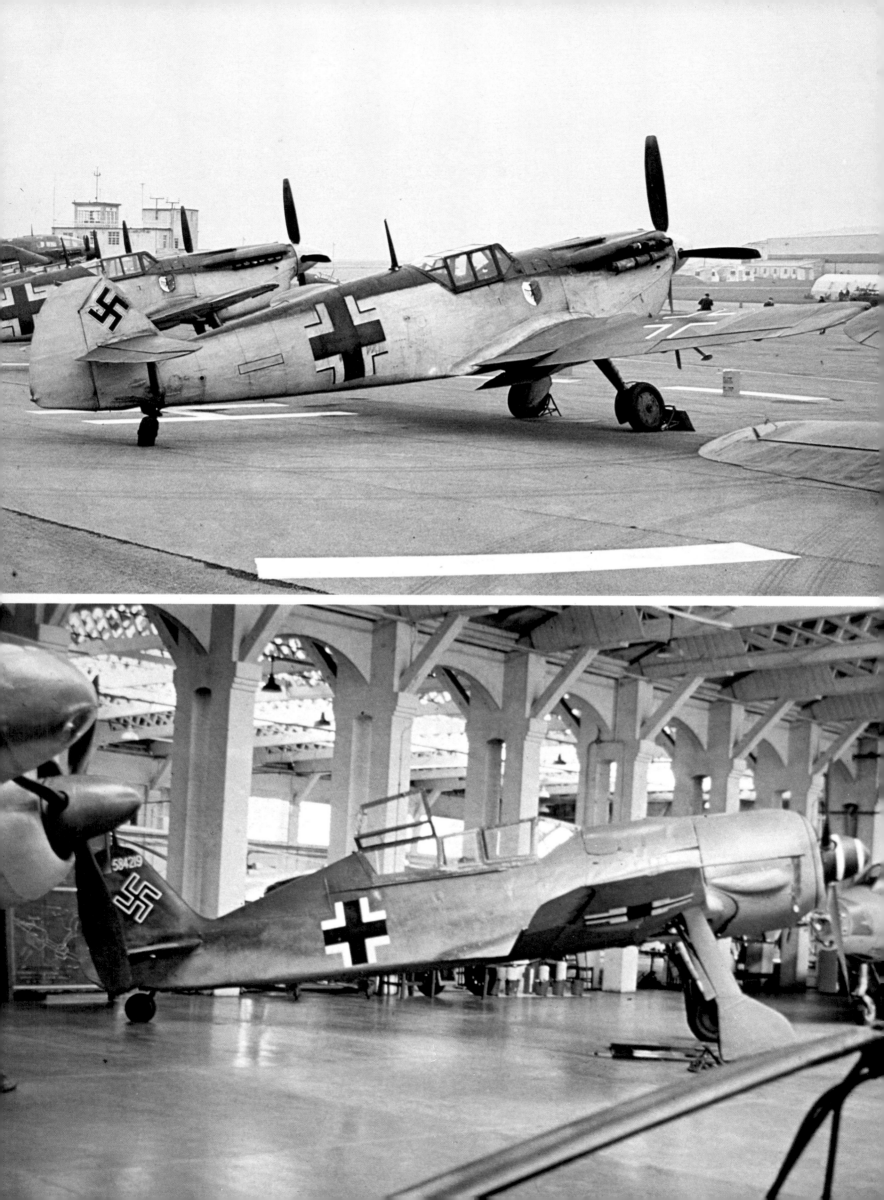

One of the world's greatest fighter aircraft was the German Bf 109 (**57** above left), designed by Willy Messerschmitt and first revealed to the public at the 1936 Olympic Games, held in Berlin.

Major production version was the Bf 109G which, with its Daimler-Benz DB 605A engine, had a maximum speed of 387 mph (623 km/h) at 23,000 ft (7,000 m). As a bomber interceptor the Bf 109G-6, armed with two MG 131 machine guns, a single MK 108 30-mm cannon firing through the propeller shaft and two MG 151 20 under-wing guns, took heavy toll of USAAF bombers on daylight raids over Germany.

One of the most outstanding radial-engined fighter aircraft ever built was the German Focke-Wulf Fw 190 (**58** below left), designed by a team under the direction of Kurt Tank.

When the first Fw 190A-1s of 6/JG 26 clashed with Spitfires on 27 September 1941, it was realized that the new German fighter had the advantage both in speed and manoeuvrability.

Towards the end of the Second World War a most dramatic and revolutionary aircraft was occasionally seen over Germany. This was the Messerschmitt Me 163B *Komet* (**59** top right), a tailless, rocket-powered interceptor.

Making its take-off run on a jettisonable trolley, the *Komet* had a maximum powered endurance of about eight minutes before the liquid propellants for its Walter rocket-engine were exhausted. Landing, on an extendable skid and tailwheel, was fraught with peril. The type had little operational success.

First turbine-powered aircraft to enter service with the *Luftwaffe* was the Messerschmitt Me 262A-1a *Schwalbe* (Swallow) (**60** centre right) which first entered full operational service with the *Kommando Nowotny* on 3 October 1944.

Its operational success, in the closing stages of the Second World War, was disappointing. If it had been introduced much earlier, instead of being delayed by Adolf Hitler's insistence that it should be developed as a bomber, the Me 262 might well have proved a most formidable adversary.

Unpleasant to fly, was the *Luftwaffe* verdict on the Heinkel He 162 *Salamander* (**61** below right) jet fighter that entered service too late to have any influence on the Second World War.

The He 162A-2, with one BMW 109-003E-1 or E-2 turbojet of 1,760 lb (800 kg) thrust, mounted above the fuselage, had a maximum level speed of 522 mph (835 km/h) at 20,000 ft (6,000 m).

Post-war development of fighter aircraft in Continental Europe has been similar to that in Britain and the United States.

One of the most successful in France has been the Dassault (now Dassault-Breguet) *Mirage* III, which has been built in many versions. One of the most interesting is illustrated, the *Mirage* III-V (**62** above), an experimental VTOL prototype, which uses eight Rolls-Royce RB.162 lift-jets for the take-off and landing phase.

Posed with the identical 'sweep-or-not-to-sweep' problem, Dassault elected to use the variable-geometry concept for an experimental fighter designated Mirage G.

The illustrations show the Mirage G8 with wings unswept (**63** above right) and swept (**64** below right), and it is reported to have exceeded a speed of Mach 2 in the latter configuration. Intended to offer supersonic performance at sea level, the development of this fighter aircraft was continuing in 1972.

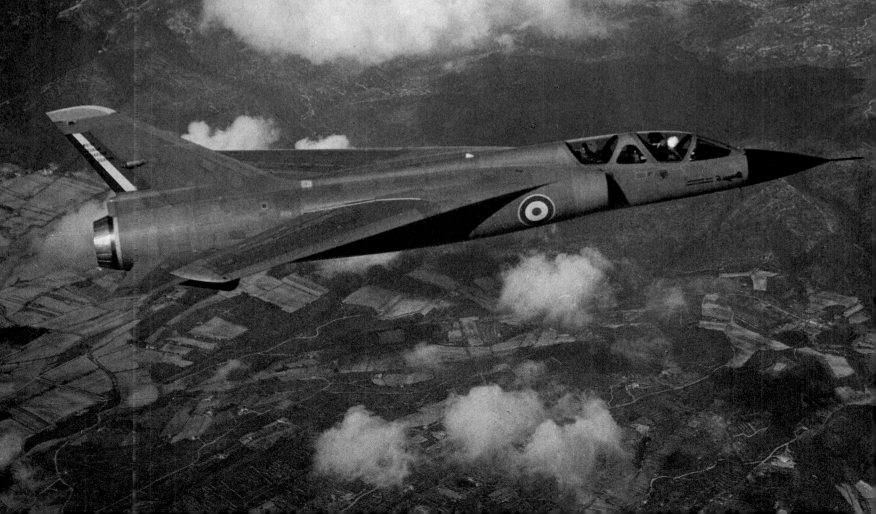

In Sweden the Saab-Scania company, as it is now known, has designed and has in production two superb Mach 2 fighter aircraft, under the designations Saab 35 *Draken* and Saab 37 *Viggen*.

The former is a single-seat all-weather fighter already in service with both Sweden and Denmark, and *Drakens* will also be in operation with the air force of Finland in 1974–5. The illustration shows two J 35 *Drakens* (**65** above) silhouetted against the setting sun, Sidewinder missiles beneath their slim fuselages.

The Saab AJ 37 *Viggen* (**66** above right) shows clearly the unusual configuration of this all-weather attack aircraft. Canard foreplanes fitted with trailing-edge flaps and rear-mounted delta wing provide excellent STOL (short take-off and landing) characteristics.

Multi-purpose aircraft are valuable to a country like Sweden, and Saab-Scania have developed an all-metal twin-jet machine known as the Saab 105 (**67** right) to fill this role.

Its duties in the Swedish Air Force include training, liaison, reconnaissance and attack. In this latter role it can carry a wide variety of armament on under-wing attachment points.

Bombers

One of the most outstanding bomber aircraft to serve with the RAF in the between-wars period was the Hawker *Hart* (**68** below), the prototype of which (J 9052) first flew in June 1928.

Powered by a single 525 hp Rolls-Royce Kestrel IB, the *Hart* had a maximum speed of 172 mph (276 km/h) at 10,000 ft (3,050 m), proving so fast that it could outpace contemporary fighters. In the 1930 Air Exercises, for example, the defending Siskin fighters tried in vain to catch them.

The *Hart* was eventually displaced by a developed version known as the *Hind*, this latter machine being the last biplane bomber of the RAF's light bomber squadrons.

The Vickers *Wellington* bomber provided the mainstay of Bomber Command's night attacks on Germany in the early stages of the Second World War. To the extent that at one period it equipped no fewer than 21 squadrons, and when the first 1,000-bomber raid was mounted against Cologne, in May 1942, more than half of the aircraft involved were 'Wimpeys', as the *Wellington* was affectionately known.

The mighty, four-engined bombers that were to supersede it, the *Halifax*, *Stirling* and *Lancaster*, all originated from a pre-war Air Ministry specification. Almost certainly the most famous of these was the Avro *Lancaster* (**69** right), and the first of Bomber Command's squadrons to be equipped with the type in early 1942 was No 44, based at Waddington, Lincs.

Lancasters will forever be associated in the mind with such epic events as No 617 Squadron's attack on the Mohne and Eder dams and the sinking of the German battleship *Tirpitz*, and as carriers of the 22,000 lb 'Grand Slam' bomb.

First jet bomber to be built in Britain, and the first to serve with the RAF, was the English Electric *Canberra*.

High speed and fighter-like manoeuvrability meant that it, like the much earlier de Havilland *Mosquito*, had no need for defensive armament.

First flown on 23 April 1950, it was built in large quantities for Bomber Command, and it was not long before this exceptional aircraft began to notch up a few records. Most significant was the World Height Record of 65,889 ft (20,083 m) by an Olympus-engined *Canberra* (WD 952) in August 1955.

The *Canberra* illustrated (**70** above left) is in the striking insignia of the Venezuelan Air Force.

To meet the need for long-range high-altitude heavy bomber aircraft, capable of carrying nuclear weapons, the Avro *Vulcan* (**71** centre left), along with the Handley Page *Victor* and Vickers *Valiant*, was developed in accordance with an Air Ministry specification that originated in 1947. The prototype *Vulcan* first flew on 30 August 1952.

The *Vulcan* was the first large bomber in the world to have a delta-wing planform, selected for good load-carrying capabilities, high sub-sonic speed at high altitude and long range. At the height of its career in the mid-sixties, it was one of the most formidable strategic attack aircraft in the world.

Contemporary with the *Vulcan* was the Handley Page *Victor*, designed to fulfil the same specification of the 'V' bomber programme. Its configuration was very different, for it featured a graceful crescent wing.

The first production *Victor* flew for the first time on 1 February 1956, and these aircraft fulfilled both a strategic bomber and reconnaissance role.

Like many large bomber aircraft whose role has been usurped by long-range ballistic missiles, *Victors* have been converted to flying fuel tankers. The illustration (**72** right) shows an early *Victor* in white anti-radiation paint scheme.

The German bomber force at the beginning of the Second World War comprised, for its day, a formidable trio: the Dornier Do 17, Heinkel He 111 and Junkers Ju 88. All three had graceful lines, probably originating from their mutual clandestine evolution as civil transport aircraft, in a country forbidden to build military aeroplanes.

Few British readers will forget the ominous throb-throb of the He 111s' (**73** below left) unsynchronized engines as, night after night during the winter of 1940/41, they introduced and maintained a new kind of horror for UK civilians.

America's USAAC had been a little ahead of Britain in specifying their need for a four-engined bomber, and the prototype Boeing Model 299 designed to meet this requirement flew for the first time on 28 July 1935.

Before it entered service, equipping initially the 2nd Bombardment Group, Boeing registered the trade mark *Flying Fortress* for this aircraft, to emphasize its heavy defensive armament.

So originated the B-17 *Flying Fortress* which, together with the four-engined Consolidated *Liberator*, was the mainstay of the USAAC (and later USAAF) bomber forces in all theatres throughout the duration of the Second World War.

The illustration shows a B-17F (74 above) of which well over 3,000 were built. This particular variant of the *Fortress* will always be remembered for the spectacular daylight raids on German factories at Schweinfurt, when losses in two raids totalled 120 aircraft.

The requirement for a bigger and better *Fortress,* a 'Hemisphere Defense Weapon' as the official requirement put it, resulted in the Boeing B-29 *Superfortress* (**75** above).

It was aircraft of this type which initiated the highly successful low-level night incendiary attacks on Japan when, on 9 March 1945, they attacked Tokyo with terrifying results.

And it was, of course, the B-29 *Enola Gay* which dropped the world's first operational atomic bomb on Hiroshima. Devastating in its destructive effect, it is surprising that final deaths were less than those caused in the initial incendiary attack on Tokyo.

Bomber of the future for the USAF is that being developed by North American Rockwell, the B-1 strategic bomber depicted in the artist's illustration (**79** left).

With a maximum take-off weight of nearly 180 tons, the B-1 is expected to fly at about Mach 2·2 at 50,000 ft (15,240 m) and have an unrefuelled range of 6,100 miles (9,800 km).

Unusual feature is its four-man crew compartment that, in emergency, will serve as an escape module. Blasted free of the airframe by explosive devices, it will be lowered to ground level by three Apollo-type parachutes.

Boeing's B-52 *Stratofortress* (**77** top) is best described as a 'big brother' of its predecessor, the B-47, retaining the same type of flexible wing.

In 1958 it represented the cornerstone of the West's deterrent policy, with the ability to carry nuclear weapons to any target in the world. The penultimate variant, the B-52G, demonstrated the range potential of the type when, in December 1960, an aircraft of the 5th Bombardment Wing flew 10,000 miles (16,093 km) in 19 hrs 45 mins.

Tail-first aeroplanes always seem to look odd, but it is convention rather than aerodynamic principle that has sited the tail unit of most aircraft at the back.

Biggest and fastest of all the tail-first projects was the experimental XB-70A *Valkyrie* (**78** above right) built by North American in the US. Intended to supersede the B-52, it was able to cruise for prolonged periods at a speed of Mach 3 (over 2,000 mph: 3,220 km/h at 70,000 ft: 21,300 m).

The first swept-wing jet bomber to be built in quantity was the Boeing B-47 *Stratojet* (**76** right) that began to equip the USAF's 306th (Medium) Bomb Wing in mid-1951. At the peak of its utilization in 1957, Strategic Air Command had some 1,800 in service.

The illustration shows how the thin, flexible wing drooped when the aircraft was at rest. When under load, in flight, it flexed in the opposite direction to provide conventional dihedral.

Close-Support

Possibly no other close-support military aircraft has attained the reputation gained by the Junkers Ju 87 (**80** below) with which Germany mounted the combined air/army/armour *Blitzkreig* that initially swept all before it in the opening stages of the Second World War.

It was, reputedly, developed at the instigation of Ernst Udet, who had been enthused by a Curtiss *Helldiver* demonstration in the US. Initial deployment in Poland created a myth of invincibility and horrifying power. This was soon destroyed when the *Stukas* encountered the *Hurricane* and *Spitfire* in the Battle of Britain.

British wartime version of the close-support aircraft was the Westland *Lysander* (**81** right), a STOL aeroplane intended primarily for artillery spotting and reconnaissance.

Nicknamed the 'Lizzie', it is best remembered by the British public for the clandestine operations of the specially-equipped *Lysander* IIIs. These were employed on the hazardous task of dropping and picking up agents in the fields of Nazi-held France.

To meet a US Navy requirement for a light armed reconnaissance aircraft, North American Rockwell produced their OV-10A *Bronco* (**82** below right), and the first production machine flew on 6 August 1967. It subsequently entered service with the US Marine Corps and USAF.

Able to carry a maximum weapon load of 3,600 lb (1,633 kg), the *Bronco* has proved valuable for Forward Air Control (FAC) operations in South-East Asia.

Forward Air Controllers have the task of policing regular areas, and thus acquire a detailed knowledge of their own 'beat'. If a situation develops that needs land or air action, they can call for helicopters to bring in troops, or direct strike aircraft to blast enemy positions.

Civil Transport

The greatest revolution in civil transport aircraft came in 1933 when the Boeing Company in America introduced their Model 247 (**83** right).

Less well-known than some of the aircraft that superseded it, the 247 was the progenitor of the modern airliner. A well streamlined low-wing monoplane, powered by two 550 hp Pratt & Whitney radial engines, it had retractable landing gear to reduce drag in flight and was the first transport aircraft to have a de-icing system for wings and tail unit. Variable-pitch propellers gave maximum efficiency for take-off and cruising flight, and control surface trim-tabs enabled the pilot to 'balance' the aircraft so that an automatic pilot could control the machine for long periods. It was also the first twin-engined monoplane airliner able to climb with a full load on the power of only one engine.

The Boeing 247, which entered service with United Air Lines in America in March 1933, sparked off a travel revolution. Approached by Transcontinental and Western Air (TWA) for a competitive transport aircraft, the Douglas Aircraft Company produced their DC-1 prototype, that was to lead to the ubiquitous DC-3 *Dakota,* which first flew in 1935 and still serves with many airlines.

But, for intercontinental services, it was still the age of the flying-boat, and it was not until the end of the Second World War that a new era of civil aviation began, resulting from the long-range transport aircraft developed to meet wartime needs.

The United States held the best cards in this post-war deal for, involved in combat remote from their own shores, they had concentrated on developing long-range aircraft.

Inevitably, as at the end of the First World War, many converted military types served as early post-war civil transports. But there were also some that were direct developments of military aircraft, such as the Boeing 307 *Stratoliner* sired by the B-17 *Flying Fortress,* and the Boeing 377 *Stratocruiser* (**84** below) which Pan American introduced on the North Atlantic route in 1949.

The *Stratocruiser* set completely new standards of air travel and, significantly, the three airlines that equipped originally with this type gained a lead over other transatlantic operators which they have retained to this day.

With the scene set for an expansion of air travel for peace, the first of the post-war designs began to appear.

Amongst the superb piston-engined aircraft which emerged, the Lockheed *Super Constellation* (**85** bottom) was first introduced on transatlantic services by the Dutch carrier KLM in 1953.

The 'Connie' is typical of the final stage of development of the long-range piston-engined transports that preceded the jet age. Providing safe and comfortable travel, the combined fleets of piston-engined types, which included also the Boeing 377, Douglas DC-7C and Lockheed L.1649A *Starliner,* carried more than a million passengers across the Atlantic in their last full year of operations.

While the piston-engined airliners were plying the Atlantic route, a revolutionary new aircraft was being developed in Britain. This was the pioneering *Comet* 1 which, when it entered service on BOAC's London–Johannesburg route on 2 May 1952, inaugurated the world's first jet airliner service.

Tragically, three of these aircraft were lost—two in inexplicable circumstances—and the *Comet* 1 was grounded.

Fortunately for the British aircraft industry they had some reserves in the field, in the form of the economical turboprop-powered Vickers *Viscount* and Bristol *Britannia* (**86** below). When the latter was put on BOAC's London–New York service in December 1957, carrying a maximum of 134 economy-class passengers, it proved to be a winner both for the airline and the British aircraft industry.

The failure of the *Comet* 1 had been one of the most bitter blows suffered by the British aircraft industry, and for the de Havilland Aircraft Company in particular.

However, both had sufficient confidence in the fundamental design to go ahead with an advanced version designated *Comet* 4 (**87** below right). Painstaking detective work by scientists and engineers had established that the *Comet* 1s had suffered metal fatigue, causing explosive decompression of the pressurized fuselage.

Airframe constructors around the world learned valuable lessons from this investigation, and on 4 October 1958 *Comet* 4s of BOAC (G-APDB and G-APDC) made simultaneous crossings of the North Atlantic, in opposite directions.

The *Comet* 4 was just too late for Britain. By the time it entered service the American industry had made good lost time and Boeing's Model 707 was ready for service. The illustration (**88** right) shows Boeing's famous 707–80 prototype, which was presented ultimately to the Smithsonian Air and Space Museum, ranking as one of aviation's twelve most significant aeroplanes.

Powered by four turbojet engines the long-range 707-320C can carry up to 202 passengers and has provided safe, fast and comfortable jet travel around the world. Its success can be measured by the fact that no fewer than 859 had been delivered by 1 June 1972.

The youthful airlines of the 1920–30 era were, in the main, carrying their passengers in then-conventional biplanes. But even in those early days came the first examples of the far more efficient cantilever-wing monoplanes.

One of the most enduring of these, and, therefore, worthy of mention, has been the Ford Tri-motor (**89** overleaf), first produced in America in 1926. Perhaps better known by its colloquial name of the "Tin Goose", examples of this remarkable aeroplane are still in use.

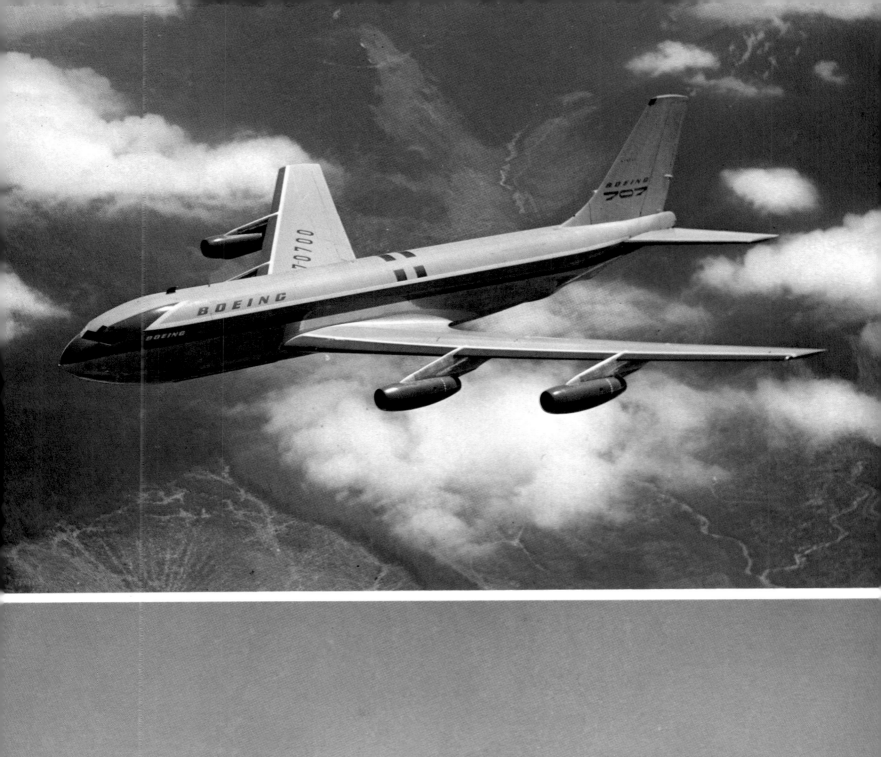

Boeing's old rival, the Douglas Aircraft Company, were not slow to follow in producing examples of the new turbojet-powered airliners that currently dominate the civil transport scene.

Illustrated are the DC-8 (**90** right) and DC-9 (**91** left). A total of 556 of the former were delivered before the production

line closed in early 1972, and a total of 649 DC-9s had been
delivered by 1 February 1972. This latter figure includes a
variant, the C-9A for the 375th Aeromedical Wing of the

Lest it should be thought that the Boeing and Douglas companies have dominated the American jet airliner scene, to the exclusion of all others, our illustrations show the graceful lines of the Convair 880 (**92** above) and Convair 990A *Coronado* (**93** top). This latter aircraft was one of the first to introduce turbofan engines, pointing the way to the quieter, cleaner jet engines of the 'seventies.

Manufacturers in Continental Europe have not stood back aghast at this development of jet transports, but have sought to enter this potentially lucrative market.

France produced one of the most successful contenders in the form of the Sud-Aviation *Caravelle* (**94** top right), a short-haul airliner with a new feature. Its turbojet engines were mounted in pods on each side of the rear fuselage providing, in addition to aerodynamic advantages, a far quieter cabin environment for its passengers. An immediate success, it soon dominated short-haul routes throughout Europe.

Other nations soon followed the French lead, bringing into service the Russian Tu-134 (**95** centre right), and BAC *One Eleven* (**96** bottom right), each having two engines.

The Hawker Siddeley *Trident* (**97** left) which has three
engines, has, like the Tu-134 (**95**) and BAC *One Eleven* (**96**)
proved highly successful on short-haul routes.

A long-range civil transport featuring rear-mounted
engines emerged when the British Aircraft Corporation introduced the VC10 (**98** above). The prototype (G-ARTA) flew
for the first time on 29 June 1962, powered by four Rolls-
Royce Conway turbofan engines.

A developed version, the Super VC10, able to accommodate up to 174 economy-class passengers, has a maximum
range of 4,720 miles (7,600 km).

On 9 February 1969 the Boeing Company announced the first flight of the first wide-bodied civil transport, the Boeing 747 (**99** top left), soon known universally as the 'jumbo jet'.

Everything about it was giant-sized, including the 200,000,000 cu ft (5,663,400 m³) single-roofed factory in which to build it; some 20,000 people involved initially on the project; and the astronomic production costs.

It was all justified. When the four 43,500 lb (17,730 kg) thrust turbofan engines lifted a Pan American 747 into the air for the first transatlantic crossing, on 22 January 1970, a new era in jet travel had been initiated.

It was inevitable that both Douglas and Lockheed would follow the pioneering effort of the Boeing Company.

First came the Douglas DC-10 Series 10, able to accommodate up to 380 economy-class passengers on domestic routes, and this made its first passenger flight with American Airlines on 5 August 1971. It was followed by the intercontinental-range Series 20, which flew for the first time on 28 February 1972.

Lockheed's L-1011 TriStar (**100** above left), powered by Rolls-Royce RB.211 high-by-pass ratio turbofan engines, made its first flight on 16 November 1970, and its first revenue flight, for Eastern Air Lines, was made on 26 April 1972.

The history of air transportation has demonstrated, quite convincingly, that passengers elect to fly in the type of aircraft which provides the fastest time over a particular route.

This is not surprising for, after all, most people travel by air with one object in mind—to get from A to B as quickly as possible—and this applies both for business and pleasure.

It was, therefore, but a matter of time before airframe manufacturers turned to the design of supersonic transports (SSTs) for airline use.

In Europe, late in 1962, British Aircraft Corporation and Sud-Aviation in France agreed to collaborate on design and construction of an SST, in due course to become known as *Concorde*.

The American industry was not slow to appreciate the sales potential of such an aircraft and, in 1967, the Boeing Company won a design competition and were all set to produce two prototypes of its Model 2707. Five years in

arrears of *Concorde's* beginnings, a decision was made to build a far larger, faster aircraft. Regrettably, a financial recession in the industry brought an end to the project.

Russia, too, decided to build an SST, similar in size and speed to the *Concorde* and this, the Tu-144 (**101** top right) stole the limelight by making the first flight on 31 December 1968.

The French-built *Concorde* 001 prototype made its first flight on 2 March 1969, the British-built 002 (**102** above right) on 9 April 1969.

The SSTs are bedevilled by problems above and beyond the mere technical: but in the final analysis there can be little doubt that aircraft of this kind will, one day, be the 'Queens' of the world's air routes.

Far removed from the glamour of the 'jumbo-jets' and the SSTs, there is a whole range of civil transports of all shapes and sizes that, as routine, travel the airlanes of the world carrying people and cargo.

Typical of medium-sized airliners of the 'sixties are the Dutch-built Fokker F.27 *Friendship* (**103** above), a 40/52-seater for short/medium-range traffic, and the Handley Page *Herald* (**104** below) and Hawker Siddeley HS 748 (**105** right)

of much the same class. All three utilize economical Rolls-Royce Dart turboprop power plants.

The *Friendship* has enjoyed considerable success, with well over 500 sales, and late versions of this popular airliner were still available in early 1973. In America, Fairchild Hiller also built the type, under the designation FH.227, and when their production line closed down more than 200 aircraft had been sold.

Air forces, too, have need for medium-range modern transport aircraft, to carry personnel, spares and urgent supplies from base to base.

In the US, North American Aviation produced an attractive utility aircraft for the USAF to meet this sort of requirement and, under the designation T-39 (**106** above) it flew for the first time on 16 September 1958.

Subsequently, civil versions were marketed under the name *Sabreliner,* the Series 60 of which, for example, can accommodate a crew of two and up to 10 passengers.

To meet a similar Canadian requirement, de Havilland Canada developed the DHC-5 *Buffalo* (**107** centre left) STOL utility transport.

Evolved from their earlier *Caribou,* it is considerably larger than the T-39 and can accommodate a crew of three and up to 41 fully-equipped troops. It flew for the first time on 9 April 1964, and it is an aircraft of this type that is being converted for an ACLS test-bed (**142**) by Bell Aerospace.

At the other extreme of the military transport requirement comes Lockheed's C-5A *Galaxy,* the largest military transport yet known to have been flown.

With a main freight deck that is 144

ft 7 in (44·07 m) long, 19 ft (5·79 m) high, and with a head clearance of 13 ft 6 in (4·11 m), the *Galaxy* can carry nearly 120 tons of freight. Its take-off weight can exceed 340 tons and its four General Electric turbofan engines can hurtle this mammoth vehicle through the air at a maximum level speed of 571 mph (919 km/h) at 25,000 ft (7,600 m).

You would not, of course, be surprised to see this monster disgorge such items as tanks, missiles and helicopters from its vast cargo holds. The illustration is of the prototype C-5 (**108** below left) which first flew on 30 June 1968.

Many transport aircraft developed originally to meet military requirements have, subsequently, been produced in commercial versions.

Lockheed's C-130 *Hercules* (**109** below right) was designed to meet a specification issued by the USAF Tactical Air Command in 1951. Highly successful, it has been built in large quantities and serves with many of the world's air forces.

Hercules commercial transports, which have an L 100 series designation, have been in service for a number of years. Largest of these, the L 100-30 (**110** above right), which entered service in 1970, can lift a maximum payload of more than 23 tons.

To provide for air transport of large items used in America's space programmes, Aero Spacelines developed and constructed a series of transport aircraft for outsize cargoes.

The *Guppy*-201 illustrated (**111** above) utilizes the lower fuselage, wings, tail unit and cockpit of a Boeing 377/C-97, portions of the lower fuselage of several aircraft being joined to provide a larger cabin. This particular aircraft is operated for Airbus Industrie, and is employed to carry major components of the A-300B Airbus and *Concorde* SST from various points of manufacture in Europe to assembly facilities at Toulouse, France.

One must not overlook the small passenger carrying aircraft used as feeder-liners or business aircraft.

The former category is used to provide local services, as well as to feed passengers from minor to major airports. The Britten-Norman *Islander* (**112** top right) is a good example, accommodating a pilot and up to nine passengers in this role,

but it can also meet the needs of the latter category with installation of special executive layouts. Powered by 260 hp piston-engines, the *Islander* has a maximum sea level speed of 170 mph (273 km/h) and range of 717 miles (1,153 km) at 75 per cent power.

Designed specifically for the business aircraft category is the Hawker Siddeley HS 125 (**113** above), which accommodates a crew of two and from six to twelve passengers. As a fast, economical transport, it is apparent that it can meet also

the feeder-liner requirement. Powered by two Rolls-Royce Bristol Viper turbojet engines, the HS 125 is in a very different speed class, the Series 600 having a maximum operating speed of 345 mph (555 km/h) IAS.

In ending our examination of the transport scene, it is interesting to take a final look at the *Hercules* in another role, as a tanker. This KC-130 F (**114** overleaf) of the US Marine Corps is seen suckling two Skyhawks of the same service.

Seaborne

Seaborne aircraft, both civil and military, have always held special appeal for aviation enthusiasts. Furthermore, time was when they seemed to offer greater built-in factors of safety for civil airlines for, after all, seven-tenths of the world's surface is covered by water.

Trans-oceanic crossings needed long-range aircraft that would be heavier than landplanes of the era and which, in any event, would require non-existent long runways to get them into the air. Vast stretches of water could be found nearly anywhere, providing almost unlimited take-off and landing areas for seaborne aircraft. Additionally, it was assumed that a flying-boat unfortunate enough to be forced down during an ocean crossing would have a far better chance of survival than a landplane.

In 1934, Britain announced introduction of the Empire Air Mail Scheme, under which all mail to or from Commonwealth countries served by Imperial Airways would be carried by air. To fulfil this requirement a fleet of four-engined flying-boats were ordered and the first of these, the Short S.23 named *Canopus*, made its first service flight on 30 October, 1936. These S.23 'Empire 'Boats' (**115** right) acquired a reputation for reliability and comfort which is unlikely to be forgotten.

The requirement for long-range aircraft to transport passengers on inter-continental flights created worldwide interest in flying-boats.

Pan American Airways appreciated the financial potential of a service across the vast expanse of the Pacific Ocean and ordered two different flying-boats; the Martin M.130 and Sikorsky S-42 (**116** below). It was an aircraft of this latter type which carried out the first survey flight from America to New Zealand, while to the Martin M.130 *China Clipper* went the honour of the first mail flight across the central Pacific.

The North Atlantic proved to be the most formidable barrier to intercontinental air traffic. Both America and Britain were anxious to establish regular services between their countries, but it was realized that little would be gained by inaugurating a route based on aircraft with only marginal range.

Proving flights were made between the two countries with flying-boats such as the Sikorsky S-42 and Short S.23. Britain even experimented with a 'pick-a-back' concept, in which a specially-constructed S.23 air-launched a seaplane named *Mercury*. Germany's Deutsche Lufthansa made trials with seaplanes of medium range which landed alongside a depot ship, which picked them up and refuelled them, before catapult-lauching them to complete the crossing.

In the end it was America that took the prize, when the 42-ton Boeing 314 (**117** right) flying-boat inaugurated the first North Atlantic passenger service on 8 July 1939. It had required nearly 36 years of aviation progress to conquer the world's oceans.

There were many useful roles that seaborne aircraft could play during the Second World War. One of particular value was air-sea rescue, which involved picking up the crew of an aircraft forced down into the sea.

In the spring of 1944 Spain acquired 12 Dornier

Do 24T-3s (**118** below) from Germany, a graceful 'boat powered by three 1,000 hp BMW engines. These were used to provide an air-sea rescue service in the Mediterannean, the Spanish machines picking up downed crews of any nationality.

Amphibious aircraft, capable of operation from both land or water, seem to offer the best of both worlds.

Grumman Corporation in America, who have a long association with all types of seaborne aircraft, produced in 1937 a general-purpose amphibian designated G-21. This was adopted by the US Navy, under the designation JFR, first entering service in 1939. Many were also built for civil use, and the Grumman *Goose* (**119** above) illustrated is popular with US conservation services.

The long-range potential of flying-boats meant that they were an extremely attractive proposition for use on maritime patrol duties.

Last of the US Navy's operational flying-boats was the Martin P5M *Marlin,* the first production model of which made its first flight on 22 June 1951. Powered by two 3,450 hp Wright radial engines, the P5M-2 *Marlin* (**120** top), of which 10 were supplied to France under the MAP, could carry up to 8,000 lb (3,629 kg) of assorted weapons.

Rotary Wing Aircraft

The concept of rotary winged aircraft has a long theoretical history stemming, possibly, from mother nature who uses spinning, winged seeds to propagate certain species of plants and trees. Be that as it may, the first helicopter-like toys recorded in history date back to the beginning of the fourteenth century, and many children of the twentieth century have played with similar toys in which string, a spiral screw or simple mechanism is employed to spin a simple four-blade rotor that flies freely in the air.

The first practical helicopter in history had been the twin-rotor Focke-Achgelis Fw-61, built and flown in Germany in 1936. The twin rotors, one on each side of the machine, overcame the problem posed by unbalanced rotors. It was not until four years later that Igor Sikorsky, in America, made the first successful flight with his single-rotor VS-300 helicopter on 13 May 1940.

In 1941, the Vought-Sikorsky Division of United Aircraft was awarded a development contract for an experimental helicopter, designated XR-4. This retained the single three-blade rotor and anti-torque rotor of the VS-300, driven through transmission shafts and gearboxes by a 165 hp Warner engine. Final service variant was the R-4B (**121** below) of which several were supplied to the Royal Air Force.

The Sikorsky S-61L (**122** bottom), shown at Los Angeles International Airport, illustrates vividly the rapid progress made in the development of efficient rotary-wing aircraft. The first flight of this commercial, non-amphibious helicopter, was made just over 20 years after the first flight of the VS-300.

Able to carry a crew of three and a maximum of 30 passengers, three S-61Ls operated by Los Angeles Airways had each exceeded 10,000 flight hours by February 1968.

One helicopter which has been around longer than any other is the Bell Model 47 (**123** above), which has been in continuous production since award of the CAA's first helicopter Approved Type Certificate in March 1946.

Production of military versions has now ended, but Bell continue to build two versions of the Model 47G for commercial applications. Seating three persons including the pilot, it has a maximum speed of 105 mph (169 km/h) and a range of around 250 miles (400 km).

The most significant period of helicopter development was signalled by the Korean War that erupted in mid-1950. In this bitter war the 'chopper' proved its ability to accomplish tasks that could be done by no other vehicle. Like putting down and picking up troops in areas completely inaccessible to surface transport or other types of aircraft. By picking up badly wounded men and hurrying them to hospital, helicopters reduced the death rate from wounds to the lowest figure in military history.

Not surprisingly, the US Army wanted bigger and better 'choppers', and in 1956 Boeing-Vertol began development of a twin-rotor turbine-powered transport helicopter for commercial and military use. Typical of this type is the CH-113 *Labrador* (**124** below left), delivered to the Royal Canadian Air Force in 1963–64 for search and rescue duties, and which has a range of over 650 miles (1,050 km).

Developed from the Boeing-Vertol Model 107, of which the RCAF *Labrador* is a variant, was the CH-47 *Chinook* (**125** top right). This is a considerably enlarged version of the Model 107, able to accommodate 33 to 44 combat troops. Despite this design capability, on one memorable occasion in Vietnam a *Chinook* evacuated no fewer than 147 refugees and their possessions in a single flight.

Demonstrating its lifting capability, helicopters of this type have recovered over 11,000 disabled aircraft—worth over $2·9 billion—from combat areas in South-East Asia, air-lifting them to repair bases.

It was soon realized that more aggressive versions of military helicopters could play an important role in operations of the kind experienced in Korea and Vietnam. In areas where guerilla-type forces were operating in small well-concealed groups, it would be comforting to have an accompanying 'chopper' that could release a hail of deadly fire, while calling up an air strike or airborne reserves.

First flown in September 1965, the Bell AH-1G *Huey Cobra* (**126** centre right) soon demonstrated its efficiency for this kind of task. Armed with a six-barrel Minigun, carried in a tactical armament turret faired into the under-surface of the front fuselage, and liberally armed with 2·75-in rockets carried beneath its stub-wings, the slim-profile *Huey* quickly became hated by its enemies.

Successful application of armed helicopters encouraged the US Army to seek a more potent derivation of the type. Increased fire power was no serious problem, but much higher speeds would increase its effectiveness and invulnerability.

In March 1966 Lockheed began development of an advanced armed helicopter, designated as the AH-56A *Cheyenne* (**127** right). Known as a compound helicopter, being provided with small low-set cantilever wings to off-load the main rotor in high-speed flight, it was designed to have a maximum level speed of 244 mph (393 km/h). Army support came to an end in 1969, and economic considerations eventually caused Lockheed to end its development programme.

In the course of time very large helicopters were developed for both civil and military requirements.

In America, Sikorsky Aircraft produced the prototype of its S-64 *Skycrane* and this flew for the first time on 9 May 1962. A military version, designated CH-54A, gained three international height records in 1965; those involving a 2,000 kg payload to a height of 28,743 ft (8,761 m) and a 1,000 kg payload to a height of 29,340 ft (8,943 m), were unbeaten in mid-1972.

Typical of civil applications is the on-site delivery of a pre-fabricated house, as shown in the illustration (**128** right).

Largest rotary-wing aircraft ever flown is the Soviet Union's Mil V-12 (**129** above), the existence of which first became known in 1969. One of the world records held by this giant was gained on 6 August 1969 when, flown by Vasily

Kolochenko, the V-12 lifted a payload of 88,636 lb (40,204·5 kg) to a height of 7,398 ft (2,255 m).

To put this achievement in more readily understandable terms, it represents a payload of over 39 tons. Perhaps more strikingly, this payload is more than double the maximum take-off weight of America's Sikorsky S-64 *Skycrane*.

One of the new military helicopters to enter service with Britain's Royal Air Force is the Anglo-French *Puma*. Designed originally to a French Army Requirement, this is an advanced medium-size helicopter able to operate by day or night in all weathers and all climates.

The SA 330 *Puma* forms one component of a joint production agreement established between Aérospatiale in France and Westland in the UK, and *Puma* HC.Mk 1s (**130** top) are in service with Nos 33 and 230 Squadrons of the RAF.

Experimental
and Research Aircraft

Exploring applications of the rotary-wing, the Fairey Aviation Company in Britain evolved in the late fifties a concept far ahead of its time, and built a prototype to prove that it would work.

This was the Fairey *Rotodyne* (**131** left), virtually a monoplane powered by two turboprop engines. Its VTOL capability was provided by a large rotor, driven by compressed-air jets located at the rotor tips. Once airborne, the *Rotodyne* flew as a conventional aircraft, its rotary-wings auto-rotating and providing only a small amount of lift. With a crew of two and 40–48 passengers, it was designed for a cruising speed of 170 mph (274 km/h) and a range in excess of 400 miles (644 km). Inadequate finance prevented the continued development of this very advanced vehicle.

At the end of the Second World War, aircraft designers were faced with a new challenge. Pilots of developed versions of aircraft such as the American P-38 *Lightning* and British *Typhoon*, both of which had maximum level speeds in excess of 400 mph (644 km/h), found that when approaching terminal velocity in a dive their aircraft began to vibrate frighteningly; it seemed almost as if they might shake to pieces. Unfortunately, some of them did: wings or tail units broke away from the main structure and many pilots died.

Because of the speed at which these aircraft were travelling, the invisible air had changed from collaborator to enemy. Unable to 'move out of the way' quickly enough, the air became compressed and formed shock-waves that hammered at the aircraft's structure. This effect—compressibility—occurs when airflow over any part of the aeroplane's structure attains the speed of sound; approximately 760 mph (1,223 km/h) at 36,000 ft (10,970 m).

The problem had to be solved, for it presented a barrier to high-speed flight offered by the new jet engines. It was not long before newspaper journalists wedded the words sound and barrier, describing the 'sound barrier' as a limiting factor in man's aspirations to realize the full potential of the gas turbine.

In America the USAF ordered a rocket-powered research aircraft from the Bell Aircraft Company. Designated X-1 (**132** top left), it was built very strongly, hopefully to survive the buffeting, and was provided with more than enough power to push it beyond the speed of sound (Mach 1·0). Flown by a USAF pilot, Charles 'Chuck' Yeager, it was air-launched at around 30,000 ft (9,145 m) from beneath the fuselage of a B-29 *Superfortress,* and in successive flights he approached nearer and nearer to Mach 1·0. On 14 October 1947, Yeager gave his little craft full power, but as it approached critical speed the buffeting was so severe that he felt he had only marginal control. Then suddenly, and unexpectedly, the buffeting stopped: 'Chuck' Yeager was through the 'barrier', into the smooth airflow of supersonic flight.

It was clear that a properly-designed aircraft could fly safely at speeds in excess of Mach 1·0. How much in excess no one knew. The Bell X-2 (**133** top right) explored the potential of swept-wings, and the Bell X-5 (**134** above left) examined the advantages or disadvantages of variable-geometry wings.

Before the USAF's research programme ended in 1969, the North American X-15-A2 (**135** above right) had carried Major Pete Knight, USAF, at a height of more than 50 miles (80 km) to earn him an astronaut's wings, and at an undreamed of speed of 4,534 mph (7,297 km/h).

Soon after Britain's first experimental jet-powered aircraft, the Gloster-Whittle E.28/39, had flown, Dr A. A. Griffith, then chief scientist at Rolls-Royce, expounded some very advanced ideas for the utilization of jet lift. During 1952 a VTOL test vehicle was built by Rolls-Royce and given the designation TMR. More popularly known as the 'Flying Bedstead', it used the power of two Nene turbojets to give vertical thrust to lift the rig. Control was provided by four downward-pointing nozzles through which engine-bleed air was ejected. The fore and aft nozzles gave control in pitch and could also be swivelled to turn the rig either way: those on each side governed roll.

The first free flight was made in 1954, and subsequent testing proved conclusively that the thrust of powerful turbojet engines would be able to lift an aircraft vertically into the air.

Following upon this research programme, Bristol Aero Engines developed their BS.53 turbofan engine with rotatable nozzles, so that thrust from the engine could be deflected downward for vertical lift, and rotated progressively to provide horizontal thrust for cruising flight. This technique is known as vectored thrust.

Hawker aircraft utilized this engine to develop a prototype V/STOL tactical fighter designated P.1127 (**136** left), which made its first transition from vertical to horizontal flight in September 1961.

The Hawker Siddeley *Harrier,* the Western world's only operational fixed-wing V/STOL strike fighter, was developed with experience gained from the P.1127. Its vertical take-off and landing capability means that it is an ideal close-support aircraft and the illustration (**137** below left) shows a typical front-line dispersal from which *Harriers* can operate. Well-concealed from prying airborne eyes, and yet at short range from the scene of action, it can quickly take off and 'harry' the enemy with a heavy load of mixed weapons. With a maximum low-level speed of approximately 737 mph (1,186 km/h), the *Harrier* is in service with the Royal Air Force and the US Marine Corps.

Helicopters, though providing true VTOL (vertical take-off and landing) flight, generally have limited range and are expensive to operate. Designers have explored many ways to provide more efficient VTOL aircraft, and considerable work has gone into research with tilt-wing designs, of which the Canadair CL-84-1 (**138** below) is an example. The basic idea is to tilt the wing so that the propellers provide vertical lift for take-off, hovering flight and landing. Once airborne, the wing is moved progressively to a conventional flight setting so that the propellers operate as normal, the wings providing the lift.

Canadair's CL-84 prototype made its first hovering flight on 7 May 1965 and its first transition to conventional flight on 17 January 1966. Three CL-84-1s with more powerful engines were ordered in February 1968 for evaluation of the aircraft's potential in a variety of military roles. A CL-84-1D version, with Lycoming T53-19A engines, modified fuselage and widertrack landing gear has been proposed as a production version.

The Boeing-Vertol Model 347 (**139 top**) is a research helicopter being developed under an advanced technology programme. It is, basically, a CH-47A *Chinook* but differs, amongst other things, by having four-blade rotors, a lengthened fuselage, retractable landing gear and more powerful engines. In its Phase 1 flight tests, completed in 1970, it demonstrated a power-limited maximum speed of 202 mph (325 km/h). In its Phase 2 configuration, a 340 sq ft (31·6m²) wing with a *g*-sensed full-span flap has been added. In continuing flight tests the effect of this wing is being evaluated to determine its reaction on rotor loading, flight characteristics and increased speed capability.

In a research programme aimed at developing a new type of landing gear that would allow military transport aircraft to operate from a variety of surfaces, such as rough fields, soft soils, swamps, water, ice and snow. Bell Aeroplane Company have been working on an Air Cushion Landing System (ACLS). The system is based on the ground effect principle, which relies upon a cushion of air as the aircraft's ground-contacting medium. This requires a large inner-tube-like attachment, known as a trunk, which protects the underside of the aircraft's fuselage. The under-surface of the trunk is perforated with hundreds of vent holes: when the trunk is inflated for taxi-ing, take-off or landing, the air escaping through these holes provides the air cushion. Following successful tests with a modified Lake LA-4 amphibian (**140 left**), Bell Aerospace is currently modifying a de Havilland Canada CC-115 *Buffalo* STOL (short take-off and landing) military transport as a test-bed aircraft.

The Dornier company, in Germany, have added their contribution to V/STOL aircraft technology, having developed in the late 1960s experimental prototypes of a transport aircraft designated Do 31 E (**141 above right**), able to accommodate a crew of two and 36 fully-equipped troops.

To provide forward propulsion and some vertical lift, two Rolls-Royce Pegasus vectored-thrust turbofan

engines were mounted beneath the wings. Major component of the vertical lift was provided by eight Rolls-Royce RB.162 lift-jets, mounted four in each wingtip pod.

As a related activity of the US space programme, very considerable research has gone into the development of wingless lifting-bodies, so-called because this type of aircraft derives its lift from the fuselage (or body) shape, and has no conventional wings.

The aim of this programme was initially to produce a craft that would perform as a spacecraft in Earth orbit, fly in Earth's atmosphere, and land conventionally at an airfield. Since the programme originated, in 1960, its scope has expanded to the concept of a space shuttle. In order to avoid wastage of the expensive hardware associated with current rocket-launched space vehicles, the space shuttle concept covers two vehicles—booster and shuttle—the former lifting the shuttle to a height of 45 miles (72·4 km) before returning to Earth and landing conventionally. The shuttle continues into orbit, possibly carrying a satellite, or may be engaged on the inspection of satellites in orbit or in ferrying crews to and from space stations.

That a wingless craft can manoeuvre safely in Earth's atmosphere and land conventionally has been amply demonstrated by lifting-bodies developed by the Martin Marietta Corporation and the Northrop Corporation in America.

A lifting body is an aerodynamic vehicle which derives its lift from the shape of its body instead of from conventional wings. Martin Marietta first explored the concept by testing three small unmanned vehicles designated SV-5P, and these were so successful that they were soon followed by the manned X-24A (**142** right).

This stocky little craft was powered by a thiokol XLR-11 turbo-rocket engine and, during 1971, attained a speed of Mach 1·62 at a height of over 71,000 ft (21,640 m) before coming into a 'normal' 160–200 mph (257–322 km/h) tricycle gear landing. A more-advanced X-24B was scheduled to begin its flight test programme in the summer of 1973.

Like the Canadair CL-84-1 (**138**), the LTV-Hiller-Ryan XC-142A (**143** overleaf) shows the results of research with the tilt-wing design. The XC-142A made its first flight in a normal mode on 29 September 1964, and the first transition from hover to horizontal flight and return on 11 January 1965. This programme was then terminated.

General Purpose Aircraft

Before turning from the activities of aircraft that operate within the Earth's atmosphere, it is important to remember specialized aircraft that perform the peaceful tasks that were the dream of the pioneers.

The helicopter has proved a magnificent life-saver in the battlefield: no less so in rescuing yachtsmen and holiday-makers from the sea, egg collectors from cliff faces and refugees from floods. Australia's Flying Doctor Service was the first to speed the sick to hospital and help.

Agricultural aircraft, that can spread weed killers or fertilizers from the air, have grown in importance. The North American Rockwell *Quail Commander* (**144** below) is a good example of the type of aircraft which has made possible great advances in sheep farming in New Zealand.

And in countries like Canada, where much of its natural wealth stems from vast forests of valuable timber, fire is the biggest enemy. Helicopters can help, putting men in close to deal with small fires, but Canadair's CL-215 amphibian is what you need to deal with large-scale outbreaks.

Most spectacular is the CL-215's water-bombing operation (**145** right), and one Canadian machine made no fewer than 306 drops in a three-day period during June 1971, dousing the fires with nearly 2 million litres of water.

Space

In Russia, in the same year that the Wright brothers recorded the world's first powered flight, Konstantin Eduardovich Tsiolkowsky designed a rocket-powered spacecraft. Not only did he specify liquid-propellants, as used by contemporary booster rockets, but he was the first to realize that a multi-stage rocket would be needed to escape from the Earth's gravitational pull.

Twenty years later, in Germany, Hermann Oberth published a book in which he explained how a rocket was able to travel in a vacuum and could be used to launch a satellite. In the same year (1923), in America, Professor Robert Goddard contrived to make an experimental liquid-propellant rocket-engine run successfully for the first time.

But the lead was taken in Germany by the *Verein für Raumschifffahrt* (VfR, Society for Space Travel), founded in 1927. Within four years they had developed rockets that could climb a mile into the sky.

One of the VfR's brighter experimenters was Wernher von Braun who, with Walter Dornberger, led the wartime team that developed the world's first ballistic missile—the German A-4 rocket (V-2). When the war ended von Braun continued his work in America and, by 1956, he and his colleagues had developed a new ballistic missile named *Redstone*.

But it was the Soviet Union that took the first mighty steps forward, announcing on 4 October 1957 that a satellite named *Sputnik* 1 was in Earth orbit. Less than four years later, on 12 April 1961, Major Yuri Gagarin became the first man to orbit the Earth in a spacecraft.

The tempo increased rapidly as both American and Russian scientists and engineers reached out towards the Moon. The Soviet *Luna* III was first to photograph the hidden side of the Moon; but America's Lunar Orbiters mapped almost 100 per cent of the lunar surface during 1966–67.

On 16 July 1969 dawned the historic day when America's Apollo 11 was blasted off the launch-pad at Kennedy Space Center, the astronaut's capsule forming but a tiny portion of the monster Saturn V booster rocket that lifted them away from Earth. Four days later man had, as predicted by Lord Byron, found his way to the Moon.

Television brought the miracle to life for men and women around the world for, as if looking over the astronauts' shoulders, they saw the lunar module *Eagle* settle on the Moon's surface, in a flurry of lunar dust.

First man to step on the Moon was Neil Armstrong, and he immediately began to photograph Edwin Aldrin as he started to make his way down *Eagle's* ladder (**146** top left). The task of this first mission, in addition to limited exploration, was to set up a number of scientific experiments. The 'solar wind' experiment, seen being deployed by Aldrin (**147** centre left), consisted of a foil sheet to absorb atomic particles emitted from the sun. Most colourful object on the Moon was undoubtedly the 'Stars and Stripes', planted with national pride near the landing site in the Sea of Tranquillity (**148** bottom left). And, like 'man Friday', they left behind a mass of strange footprints (**149** right), for explorers of future generations to ponder, as they went about the business of setting up more scientific experiments.

Apollo 17, which made a spectacular night-time blast-off from Cape Kennedy on 7 December 1972, represented the last of the Moon flights in NASA's programme, and it may be that Eugene Cernan and Dr Harrison Schmitt may be the last men to tread the Moon's surface for many years. Developing techniques may not require that men be present!

The Soviet Union has not, so far, put men on the Moon. Instead she has demonstrated some remarkable and thought-provoking achievements. *Luna* 16 soft-landed on the Moon in the Sea of Fertility on 20 September 1970, collected core samples electro-mechanically by Earth-command, blasted off the surface again, and the capsule complete with samples was recovered near Dzhezkazgan, in Soviet territory, on 24 September. Two months later, on 17 November 1970, *Luna* 17 soft-landed a self-propelled mobile exploration vehicle known as *Lunokhod* 1. Controlled by a five-man team on Earth, this strange-looking vehicle soon proved that even the first of the species could be moved for considerable distances and was able to carry out a number of scientific experiments.

Further development along these lines may mean that there will be no need for men to risk their lives in routine exploration of inhospitable planets.

Man has already achieved a great deal, and the proposed US/USSR collaboration may expand our understanding of technologies that, one day, will allow men to travel easily and safely into deep space. For the present, we must be satisfied if this development of understanding between East and West will presage an era of extended peace on Earth. Then the dreams of the 'stick and string' pioneers will have been fulfilled.

Tables of Technical Data

ILLUSTRATION NO	AIRCRAFT	TYPE	WING SPAN ft-in (m)	LENGTH OVERALL ft-in (m)	HEIGHT OVERALL ft-in (m)	POWER PLANT	MAX T-O WEIGHT lbs (kg)	MAX LEVEL SPEED mph (km/h)	PAGE NO
1	de Havilland Tiger Moth	Two-seat primary trainer	29–4 (8·94)	23–11 (7·29)	8–9½ (2·68)	1 × 130 hp de Havilland Gypsy Major IA	1,650 (748)	109 (175)	12
2	Taylor Monoplane	Single-seat light monoplane	21–0 (6·40)	15–0 (4·57)	4–10 (1·47)	1 × 38 hp JAP HA	610 (276)	105 (169)	13
3	EAA Biplane	Single-seat homebuilt biplane	20–0 (6·10)	17–0 (5·18)	6–0 (1·83)	1 × 85 hp Continental HA	1,150 (522)	125 (201)	13
4	Bede BD–4	Two/four-seat homebuilt utility monoplane	25–6 (7·77)	21–10½ (6·67)	6–2½ (1·89)	1 × 108 hp Lycoming HA	1,550 (703)	156 (251)	13
5	Aerosport Rail	Homebuilt lightweight monoplane	23–3½ (7·10)	15–9 (4·80)	6–0 (1·83)	2 × 33 hp Aerosport-Rockwell HA	710 (322)	95 (153)	14
6	Pazmany PL–I	Two-seat homebuilt monoplane	28–0 (8·53)	18–11 (5·77)	8–8 (2·64)	1 × 95 hp Continental HA	1,326 (602)	120 (193)	15
7	Cessna 172 floatplane	Four-seat cabin monoplane	35–10 (10·92)	27–0 (8·23)	9–11 (3·02)	1 × 150 hp Lycoming HA	2,220 (1,007)	108 (174)	15
8	Cessna 310	Five/six-seat cabin monoplane	36–11 (11·25)	29–3 (8·92)	10–6 (3·20)	2 × 260 hp Continental HA	5,300 (2,404)	236 (379)	16
9	Beech H18	Nine/eleven-seat cabin monoplane	49–8 (15·14)	35–2½ (10·70)	9–4 (2·84)	2 × 450 hp Pratt & Whitney RA	9,900 (4,490)	236 (379)	16
10	Beech V35B Bonanza	Four/six-seat cabin monoplane	33–5½ (10·20)	26–4½ (8·04)	7–7 (2·31)	1 × 285 hp Continental HA	3,400 (1,542)	210 (338)	17
11	Piper Tri-Pacer	Four-seat cabin monoplane	29–3 (8·90)	20–7¼ (6·28)	8–4 (2·54)	1 × 160 hp Lycoming HA	2,000 (908)	141 (226)	17
12	Avions Pierre Robin DR 253 Régent	Four/five-seat cabin monoplane	28–7¼ (8·72)	23–6¾ (7·18)	7–9½ (2·38)	1 × 180 hp Lycoming HA	2,425 (1,100)	171 (275)	19
13	Beagle B.121 Pup–150	Two/three-seat cabin monoplane	31–0 (9·45)	22–9 (6·93)	8–6 (2·59)	1 × 150 hp Lycoming HA	1,600 (725)	153 (246)	18
13	Beagle B.206. Series II	Five/eight-seat executive transport	45–9½ (13·96)	33–8 (10·26)	11–3 (3·43)	2 × 340 hp Rolls-Royce/Continental HA	7,499 (3,401)	258 (415)	18
14	Airmark/Cassutt 111M	Single-seat racing monoplane	14–11 (4·54)	16–0 (4·88)	4–3 (1·30)	1 × 95 hp Rolls-Royce/Continental HA	830 (376)	207 (333)	18
15	Bensen B 8M Gyro-Copter	Single-seat homebuilt autogyro	*20–0 (6·10)	11–4 (3·45)	6–3 (1·90)	1 × 72 hp McCulloch HA	500 (227)	85 (137)	19
16	Farrington (Air & Space) Model 18–A	Two-seat light autogyro	*35–0 (10·67)	19–10 (6·04)	9–3 (2·82)	1 × 180 hp Lycoming HA	1,800 (816)	110 (177)	19
17	Lockheed U–2	Single-seat strategic reconnaissance aircraft	80–0 (24·38)	49–7 (15·11)	13–0 (3·96)	1 × 17,000 lb st Pratt & Whitney TJ	17,270 (7,823)	528 (850)	20
18	McDonnell Douglas F–4B Phantom II	Two-seat all-weather fighter	38–5 (11·70)	58–3 (17·76)	16–3 (4·96)	2 × 17,000 lb st General Electric TJ	54,600 (24,765)	Mach 2·0 +	21
19	Lockheed SR–71A	Two-seat strategic reconnaissance aircraft	55–7 (16·95)	107–5 (32·74)	18–6 (5·64)	2 × 32,500 lb st Pratt & Whitney TJ	E 170,000 (77,110)	E Mach 3·0	21
20	Lockheed YO–3A	Single-seat quiet reconnaissance aircraft	NOT KNOWN			1 × 210 hp Continental HA	NOT KNOWN		22
21	Ryan Model 154	High-altitude reconnaissance RPV				NOT KNOWN			22
22	Ryan Model 147	Utility reconnaissance RPV				NOT KNOWN			23
23	Hawker Siddeley Nimrod MR. Mk 1	Maritime reconnaissance aircraft	114–10 (35·00)	126–9 (38·63)	29–8½ (9·01)	4 × 11,500 st Rolls-Royce Spey TF	192,000 (87,090)	575 (926)	23
24	Gloster Gladiator	Single-seat fighter	32–3 (9·83)	27–5 (8·36)	10–4 (3·15)	1 × 840 hp Bristol Mercury RA	4,750 (2,154)	253 (407)	24
25	Hawker Hurricane I	Single-seat fighter	40–0 (12·19)	31–5 (9·58)	13–1½ (4·00)	1 × 1,030 hp Rolls-Royce Merlin IL	6,600 (2,994)	316 (508)	25
26	Supermarine Spitfire VI	Single-seat fighter	40–2 (12·24)	29–11 (9·12)	——	1 × 1,415 hp Rolls-Royce Merlin IL	6,797 (3,083)	364 (586)	25
27	Fairey Swordfish	Two/three-seat carrier-based torpedo-reconnaissance	45–6 (13·87)	36–4 (11·07)	12–10 (3·91)	1 × 690 hp Bristol Pegasus RA	9,250 (4,196)	139 (224)	26
28	de Havilland Mosquito VI	Two-seat fighter/bomber	54–2 (16·51)	40–6 (12·34)	15–3 (4·65)	2 × 1,230 hp Rolls-Royce Merlins IL	22,300 (10,115)	380 (612)	26
29	Gloster Meteor F.4	Single-seat fighter	37–2 (11·33)	41–4 (12·60)	13–0 (3·96)	2 × 1,700 lb st Rolls-Royce Wellands TJ	15,175 (6,883)	585 (941)	27
30	Hawker Sea Hawk	Single-seat carrier-borne ground-attack fighter	39–0 (11·89)	39–8 (12·09)	8–8 (2·64)	1 × 5,200 lb st Rolls-Royce Nene TJ	16,200 (7,347)	560 (901)	27
31	BAC Jet Provost T. Mk 4	Two-seat primary jet trainer	36–11 (11·25)	32–5 (9·88)	10–2 (3·11)	1 × 2,500 lb st Bristol-Siddeley Viper TJ	7,400 (3,356)	410 (660)	28
32	Canadair CT–114 Tutor	Two-seat jet trainer	36–5¾ (11–13)	32–0 (9·75)	9–3¾ (2·84)	1 × 2,950 lb st General Electric TJ	11,288 (5,131)	480 (774)	28
33	Hawker Hunter F. Mk 6	Single-seat fighter	33–8 (10·26)	45–10½ (13·98)	13–2 (4·01)	1 × 10,000 lb st Rolls-Royce Avon TJ	24,000 (10,900)	715	29
34	English Electric Lightning F. Mk 1A	Single-seat all-weather fighter	34–10 (10·61)	55–3 (16·84)	19–7 (5·97)	2 × 14,430 lb st Rolls-Royce Avons TJ	——	Mach 2·0	29
35	Supermarine Scimitar	Single-seat carrier-borne fighter	37–2 (11·33)	55–4 (16·87)	15–3 (4·65)	2 × 11,250 lb st Rolls-Royce Avons TJ	40,000 (18,145)	710 (1,142)	30
36	Blackburn Buccaneer S.1	Two-seat carrier-borne low-level strike aircraft	44–0 (13·41)	63–5 (19·33)	16–3 (4·95)	2 × 7,100 lb st de Havilland Gyron Jr TJ	45,000 (20,412)	720 (1,159)	30
37	Boeing P–26A	Single-seat fighter	27–11½ (8·52)	23–7¼ (7·19)	10–0½ (3·06)	1 × 500 hp Pratt & Whitney RA	2,955 (1,340)	234 (377)	31
38	Lockheed P–38J Lightning	Single-seat fighter and long-range escort	52–0 (15·85)	37–10 (11·53)	9–10 (3·00)	2 × 1,425 hp Allison IL	21,600 (9,797)	414 (666)	31
39	Republic F 84F Thunderjet	Single-seat fighter-bomber	33–7¼ (10·24)	43–4¾ (13·23)	14–4¾ (4·39)	1 × 7,220 lb st Wright TJ	28,000 (12,701)	695 (1,118)	32–33
40	Lockheed T–33A	Two-seat advanced trainer	38–10½ (11·85)	37–9 (11·51)	11–4 (3·45)	1 × 4,600 lb st Allison TJ	11,965 (5,428)	543 (874)	34
41	North American F–86F Sabre	Single-seat fighter-bomber	37–1 (11·30)	37–6 (11·43)	14–8 (4·47)	1 × 5,970 lb st General Electric TJ	17,100 (7,756)	707 (1,138)	35
42	Lockheed F–104G Starfighter	Single-seat fighter	21–11 (6·68)	54–9 (16·69)	13–6 (4·11)	1 × 15,800 lb st General Electric TJ	28,779 (13,054)	Mach 2·2	35
43	Ling-Temco-Vought F–8A Crusader	Single-seat carrier-borne fighter	35–8 (10·87)	54–3 (16·54)	15–9 (4·80)	1 × 16,000 lb st Pratt & Whitney TJ	34,000 (15,420)	1,000 + (1,600) +	36
44, 45, 46	Ling-Temco-Vought A–7D Corsair II	Single-seat carrier-borne tactical fighter	38–9 (11·80)	46–1½ (14·06)	16–0 (4·88)	1 × 14,250 lb st Allison TJ	42,000 (19,050)	698 (1,123)	36–37
47, 48	General Dynamics F–111A	Two-seat tactical fighter-bomber	63–0 (19·20)	73–6 (22·40)	17–1½ (5·22)	2 × 21,000 lb st Pratt & Whitney TF	91,500 (41,500)	Mach 2·5	38
49	Grumman F–14A Tomcat	Two-seat carrier-borne multi-role fighter	64–1½ (19·54)	61–10½ (18·86)	16–0 (4·88)	2 × 20,600 lb st Pratt & Whitney TF	E 66,200 (30,028)	E Mach 2 +	39
50	McDonnell Douglas F–15A Eagle	Single-seat air superiority fighter	42–9¾ (13·05)	63–9¾ (19·45)	18–7¼ (5·67)	2 × 29,000 lb st Pratt & Whitney TF	E 40,000 (18,145)	E Mach 2 +	39
51	Northrop F–5E Tiger II	Single-seat tactical fighter	26–8 (8·13)	48–3¾ (14·73)	13–4½ (4·08)	2 × 5,000 lb st General Electric TJ	21,820 (9,897)	Mach 1·6	39
52, 53, 55	Lockheed P2V–5 Neptune	Land-based anti-submarine patrol bomber	102–0 (31·08)	81–7 (24·87)	28–1 (8·56)	2 × 3,250 hp Wright RA	76,152 (34,542)	341 (549)	40–43

ILLUSTRATION NO	AIRCRAFT	TYPE	WING SPAN ft-in (m)	LENGTH OVERALL ft-in (m)	HEIGHT OVERALL ft-in (m)	POWER PLANT	MAX T-O WEIGHT lbs (kg)	MAX LEVEL SPEED mph (km/h)	PAGE NO
54, 55	Lockheed P–3B Orion	Land-based anti-submarine patrol bomber	99–8 (30·37)	116–10 (35·61)	33–8½ (10·29)	4 × 4,910 shp Allison TP	134,000 (60,780)	476 (765)	41–43
56	Lockheed S–3A Viking	Carrier-borne anti-submarine aircraft	68–8 (20·93)	53–4 (16·26)	22–9 (6·93)	2 × 9,000 lb st General Electric TF	E 42,500 (19,277)	E 506 (814)	42
57	Messerschmitt Bf 109F–3	Single-seat fighter	32–6½ (9·92)	29–0¾ (8·86)	11–2 (3·40)	1 × 1,300 hp Daimler-Benz IL	6,063 (2,750)	391 (630)	44
58	Focke-Wulf FW 190 D–9	Single-seat fighter	34–5½ (10·50)	33–5¼ (10·24)	11–0¼ (3·35)	1 × 1,776 hp Junkers Jumo IL	10,670 (4,850)	426 (685)	44
59	Messerschmitt Me 163B Komet	Single-seat rocket-powered interceptor	30–7 (9·32)	18–8 (5·69)	——	1 × 3,300 lb st Walter RE	9,042 (4,110)	596 (960)	45
60	Messerschmitt Me 262A–1a Schwalbe	Single-seat fighter	41–0 (12·50)	34–9½ (10·61)	12–6¾ (3·83)	2 × 1,980 lb st Junkers Jumo TJ	14,938 (6,775)	536 (868)	45
61	Heinkel He 162 Salamander	Single-seat fighter	23–7¾ (7·20)	29–8½ (9·00)	8–4½ (2·55)	1 × 1,980 lb st BMW TJ	5,953 (2,700)	522 (835)	45
62	Dassault Mirage III–V	Experimental VTOL strike aircraft	28–7¼ (8·72)	59–0½ (18·00)	——	1 × 16,755 lb st TF 8 × 3,525 lb st TJ	29,630 (13,440)	Mach 1·35	46
63, 64	Dassault Mirage G8	Experimental variable-geometry fighter	42–8 (13·00)	55–1 (16·80)	17–6½ (5·35)	2 × 15,875 lb st SNECMA Atars TJ	E 44,092 (20,000)	Mach 2·5	47
65	Saab 35X Draken	Single-seat all-weather fighter/reconnaissance/attack	30–10 (9·40)	50–4 (15·35)	12–9 (3·89)	1 × 12,790 lb st Volvo Flygmotor Avon TJ	33,070 (15,000)	Mach 2·0	48
66	Saab AJ 37 Viggen	Single-seat all-weather attack aircraft	34–9¼ (10·60)	53–5¾ (16·30)	18–4½ (5·60)	1 × 14,770 lb st Volvo Flygmotor TF	35,275 (16,000)	Mach 2·0	49
67	Saab 105	Multi-purpose light monoplane	31–2 (9·50)	34–5 (10·50)	8–10 (2·70)	2 × 1,640 lb st Turbo-méca Aubisques TF	9,920 (4,500)	447 (720)	49
68	Hawker Hart	Two-seat light day bomber	37–3 (11·35)	29–4 (8·94)	10–5 (3·18)	1 × 525 hp Rolls-Royce Kestrel IL	4,554 (2,065)	184 (296)	50
69	Avro Lancaster I	Long-range night-bomber	102–0 (31·09)	69–6 (21·18)	20–0 (6·10)	4 × 1,460 hp Rolls-Royce Merlins IL	70,000 (31,751)	287 (462)	51
70	English Electric Canberra B.2	Light bomber	63–11½ (19·49)	65–6 (19·96)	15–7 (4·75)	2 × 6,500 lb st Rolls-Royce Avons TJ	46,000 (20,885)	517 (827)	52
71	Avro Vulcan B. Mk 2	Long-range medium bomber	99–0 (30·15)	97–1 (29·61)	26–1 (7·93)	4 × 17,000 lb st Bristol Olympus TJ	——	Mach 0·94	52
72	Handley Page Victor B.Mk 2	Medium bomber	120–0 (36·60)	114–11 (35·00)	30–1½ (9·18)	4 × 20,600 lb st Rolls-Royce Conways TJ	——	Mach 0·92	53
73	Heinkel He 111E–3	Medium-range bomber	74–1¾ (22·60)	57–5 (17·50)	14–5¼ (4·40)	2 × 1,000 hp Junkers Jumo IL	21,168 (9,600)	261 (420)	52
74	Boeing B–17E Flying Fortress	Medium bomber	103–9 (31·62)	73–10 (22·50)	19–2 (5·84)	4 × 1,200 hp Wright RA	53,000 (24,040)	317 (510)	54
75	Boeing B–29A Superfortress	Medium bomber	141–3 (43·05)	99–0 (30·18)	29–7 (9·02)	4 × 2,200 hp Wright RA	141,100 (64,000)	358 (576)	55
76	Boeing B–47E Stratojet	Medium bomber	116–0 (35·36)	109–10 (33·48)	27–11 (8·51)	6 × 6,000 lb st General Electric TJ	206,700 (93,760)	606 (975)	56
77	Boeing B–52G Stratofortress	Heavy bomber	185–0 (56·39)	157–7 (48·03)	40–8 (12·40)	8 × 11,200 lb st Pratt & Whitney TJ	480,000 (217,720)	660 (1,062)	57
78	North American XB–70A Valkyrie	Research prototype of strategic bomber	105–00 (32·00)	196–0 (59·74)	——	6 × 31,000 lb st General Electric TJ	530,000 (240,400)	Mach 3·0	57
79	North American Rockwell B–1	Strategic bomber	137–0 (41·75)	143–0 (43·58)	34–0 (10·36)	4 × 30,000 lb st General Electric TF	400,000 (181,450)	E Mach 2·2	56
80	Junkers Ju 87B–2	Close-support dive-bomber	45–3½ (13·80)	36–1 (11·00)	12–9½ (3·90)	1 × 1,200 hp Junkers Jumo IL	9,321 (4,250)	237 (380)	58
81	Westland Lysander I	Two-seat close-support aircraft	50–0 (15·24)	30–6 (9·30)	11–6 (3·51)	1 × 890 hp Bristol Mercury RA	5,920 (2,685)	229 (369)	59
82	North American OV–10A Bronco	Multi-purpose counter-insurgency aircraft	40–0 (12·19)	41–7 (12·67)	15–2 (4·62)	2 × 715 shp AiResearch TP	14,446 (6,563)	281 (452)	59
83	Boeing Model 247–D	Short/medium-range airliner	74–0 (22·56)	51–4 (16·25)	12–1¾ (3·70)	2 × 525 hp Pratt & Whitney RA	13,650 (6,197)	202 (324)	61
84	Boeing Model 377 Stratocruiser	Long-range airliner	141–3 (43·00)	110–4 (33·65)	38–3 (11·66)	4 × 2,800 hp Pratt & Whitney RA	145,800 (76,195)	375 (603)	60
85	Lockheed Super Constellation	Long-range airliner	123–0 (37·49)	113–7 (34·65)	24–9 (7·56)	4 × 3,250 hp Wright RA	133,000 (60,380)	352 (563)	60
86	Bristol Britannia Series 310	Long-range airliner	142–3½ (43·38)	124–3 (37·89)	36–8¼ (11·19)	4 × 4,120 shp Bristol Proteus TP	175,000 (79,380)	385 (616)	62
87	de Havilland Comet 4	Long-range airliner	115–0 (35·00)	111–6 (33·99)	28–4½ (8·65)	4 × 10,500 lb st Rolls-Royce Avons TJ	152,500 (69,235)	500 (800)	63
88	Boeing Model 707–320B	Long-range airliner	145–9 (44·42)	152–11 (46·61)	42–5 (12·92)	4 × 19,000 lb st Pratt & Whitney TF	333,600 (151,315)	627 (1,010)	63
89	Ford Tri-Motor 4–AT	Short-range airliner	74–0 (22·56)	49–10 (15·20)	12–8 (3·86)	3 × 300 hp Wright or Pratt & Whitney RA	10,130 (4,590)	134 (214)	64–65
90	Douglas DC–8 Super 63	Long-range airliner	148–5 (43·41)	187–5 (57·12)	42–5 (12·92)	4 × 18,000 lb st Pratt & Whitney TJ	350,000 (158,760)	600 (965)	67
91	Douglas DC–9 Series 30	Short/medium-range airliner	93–5 (28·47)	119–3½ (36·37)	27–6 (8·38)	2 × 14,000 lb st Pratt & Whitney TF	98,000 (44,450)	565 (909)	66
92	Convair 880	Medium-range airliner	120–0 (36·58)	129–4 (39·42)	36–0 (10·97)	4 × 11,200 lb st General Electric TJ	189,500 (85,950)	615 (990)	68
93	Convair 990A Coronado	Long-range airliner	120–0 (36·58)	139–5 (42·50)	39·6 (12·04)	4 × 16,100 lb st General Electric TF	244,200 (110,765)	625 (1,006)	68
94	Sud-Aviation Caravelle III	Medium-range airliner	112–6 (34·30)	105–0 (32·01)	28–7 (8·72)	2 × 11,400 lb st Rolls-Royce Avons TJ	101,413 (46,000)	500 (805)	69
95	Tupolev Tu 134A	Short/medium-range airliner	95–1¾ (29·00)	122–0 (37·10)	29–7 (9·02)	2 × 14,990 lb st Soloviev TF	103,600 (47,000)	540 (870)	69
96	BAC One-Eleven Series 500	Short/medium-range airliner	93–6 (28·50)	107–0 (32·61)	24–6 (7·47)	2 × 12,550 lb st Rolls-Royce Speys TF	104,500 (47,400)	541 (871)	69
97	Hawker Siddeley Trident 3B	Short/medium-range airliner	98–0 (29·87)	131–2 (39·98)	28–3 (8·61)	2 × 11,960 lb st Rolls-Royce Speys TF and 1 × 5,250 lb st Rolls-Royce RB.162 TJ	150,000 (68,040)	605 (972)	70
98	BAC VC10 Series 1100	Medium/long-range airliner	146–2 (44·55)	158–8 (48·36)	39–6 (12·04)	4 × 21,000 lb st Rolls-Royce Conways TF	312,000 (141,520)	Mach 0·86	71
99	Boeing Model 747–200B	Long-range airliner	195–8 (59·64)	231–4 (70·51)	63–5 (19·33)	4 × 45,000 lb st Pratt & Whitney TF	775,000 (351,540)	608 (978)	72
100	Lockheed L–1011 TriStar	Short/medium-range airliner	155–4 (47·34)	178–8 (54·35)	55–4 (16·87)	3 × 42,000 lb st Rolls-Royce TF	430,000 (195,045)	Mach 0·9	72
101	Tupolev Tu–144	Supersonic transport aircraft	90–8½ (27·65)	196–10 (60·00)	——	4 × 28,660 lb st Kuznetsov TF	395,000 (179,150)	Mach 2·37	73
102	BAC-Aérospatiale Concorde 01	Supersonic transport aircraft	84–0 (25·60)	203–11½ (62·17)	40–0 (12·19)	4 × 34,730 lb st Rolls-Royce TJ	343,500 (155,800)	Mach 2·2	73
103	Fokker F.27 Friendship Series 500	Medium-range airliner	95–2 (29·00)	82–0½ (25·01)	27–11 (8·50)	2 × 2,050 shp Rolls-Royce Darts TP	43,500 (19,730)	292 (470)	74
104	Handley Page Herald Series 200	Short/medium-range airliner	94–9 (28·88)	75–6 (23·01)	24–1 (7·34)	2 × 1,910 shp Rolls-Royce Darts TP	43,000 (19,500)	275 (443)	74
105	Hawker Siddeley HS 748 Series 2A	Short/medium-range airliner	98–6 (30·02)	67–0 (20·42)	24–10 (7·57)	2 × 2,280 shp Rolls-Royce Darts TP	44,495 (20,182)	278 (448)	75
106	North American T–39A	Utility trainer or transport	44–5 (13·54)	43–9 (13·34)	16–0 (4·88)	2 × 3,000 lb st Pratt & Whitney TJ	17,760 (8,055)	595 (958)	76
107	de Havilland Canada DHC–5 Buffalo CC–115	STOL utility transport	96–0 (29·26)	79–0 (24·08)	28–8 (8·73)	2 × 3,055 shp General Electric TP	49,200 (22,316)	261 (420)	76

ILLUSTRATION NO	AIRCRAFT	TYPE	WING SPAN ft-in (m)	LENGTH OVERALL ft-in (m)	HEIGHT OVERALL ft-in (m)	POWER PLANT	MAX T-O WEIGHT lbs (kg)	MAX LEVEL SPEED mph (km/h)	PAGE NO
108	Lockheed C–5A Galaxy	Heavy logistics transport aircraft	222–8½ (67·88)	247–10 (75·54)	65–1½ (19·85)	4 × 41,000 lb st General Electric TF	764,500 (346,770)	571 (919)	76
109	Lockheed C–130E Hercules	Medium/long-range combat transport	132–7 (40·41)	97–9 (29·78)	38–3 (11·66)	4 × 4,050 shp Allison TP	175,000 (79,380)	384 (618)	77
110, 114	Lockheed L–100–30	Medium/long-range commercial transport	132–7 (40·41)	112–8½ (34·35)	38–3 (11·66)	4 × 4,050 shp Allison TP	155,000 (70,308)	377 (607)	77, 80–81
111	Aero Spacelines Guppy–201	Heavy transport aircraft	156–3 (47·62)	143–10 (43·84)	48–6 (14·78)	4 × 4,912 shp Allison TP	170,000 (77,110)	242 (390)	78
112	Britten-Norman Islander	Feeder-line transport	49–0 (14·94)	35–7¾ (10·86)	13–8¾ (4·18)	2 × 260 hp Lycoming HA	6,300 (2,857)	170 (273)	79
113	Hawker Siddeley HS 125 Series 600	Light executive transport	47–0 (14–33)	50–5¾ (15–39)	17–3 (5·26)	2 × 3,750 lb st Rolls-Royce Bristol Vipers TJ	25,000 (11,340)	345 (555)	79
115	Short S.23 C-Class	Medium-range flying-boat transport	114–0 (34·75)	88–0 (26·82)	31–9¾ (9·68)	4 × 790 hp Bristol Pegasus RA	40,500 (18,375)	200 (322)	82
116	Sikorsky S–42	Medium-range flying-boat transport	114–2 (34·80)	67–8 (20·93)	17–4 (5·28)	4 × 700 hp Pratt & Whitney RA	38,000 (17,250)	182 (291)	82
117	Boeing Model 314–A Clipper	Long-range flying-boat transport	152–0 (46·36)	106–0 (32·33)	20–4½ (6·22)	4 × 1,600 hp Wright RA	84,000 (38,136)	210 (336)	83
118	Dornier Do 24T–3	Patrol flying-boat	88–7 (27·00)	72–2½ (22·00)	18–10½ (5·75)	3 × 1,000 hp BMW–Bramo RA	39,249 (17,800)	211 (340)	83
119	Grumman Goose	General utility amphibian	49–0 (14·95)	38–4 (11·70)	15–0 (4·57)	2 × 400 hp Pratt & Whitney RA	8,000 (3,629)	201 (323)	84
120	Martin P5M–2 Marlin	Patrol flying-boat	118–2 (36·02)	100–7 (30·66)	32–8½ (9·97)	2 × 3,450 hp Wright RA	85,000 (38,555)	251 (404)	84
121	Sikorsky R–4B	General-purpose helicopter	*38–0 (11·58)	48–2 (14·68)	12–5 (3·78)	1 × 180 hp Warner RA	2,535 (1,150)	75 (121)	85
122	Sikorsky S–61L	All-weather helicopter airliner	*62–0 (18·90)	72–7 (22·12)	17–0 (5·18)	2 × 1,500 shp General Electric TS	19,000 (8,620)	146 (235)	85
123	Bell Model 47G–5A	Three-seat general utility helicopter	*37–1½ (11·32)	43–7½ (13·30)	9–3¾ (2·84)	1 × 265 hp Lycoming HA	2,850 (1,293)	105 (169)	86
124	Boeing-Vertol CH–113 Labrador	Transport helicopter	*50–0 (15·24)	83–4 (25·40)	16–8½ (5–09)	2 × 1,250 shp General Electric TS	21,400 (9,707)	157 (253)	86
125	Boeing-Vertol CH–47B Chinook	Medium transport helicopter	*60–0 (18·29)	99–0 (30·18)	18–7 (5·67)	2 × 2,850 shp Lycoming TS	40,000 (18,144)	144 (232)	87
126	Bell AH–1G Huey Cobra	Combat helicopter	*44–0 (13·41)	52–11½ (16·14)	13–5½ (4·10)	1 × 1,400 shp Lycoming TS	9,500 (4,309)	219 (352)	87
127	Lockheed AH–56A Cheyenne	Combat helicopter	*51–3 (15·62)	60–1 (18·31)	13–8½ (4·18)	1 × 3,925 shp General Electric TS	18,300 (8,300)	244 (393)	87
128	Sikorsky S–64 Skycrane	Heavy flying-crane helicopter	*72–0 (21·95)	88–6 (26·97)	18–7 (5·67)	2 × 4,500 shp Pratt & Whitney TS	42,000 (19,050)	127 (204)	89
129	Mil Mi–12 (V–12)	Heavy general-purpose helicopter	*114–10 (35·00)	121–4½ (37·00)	41–0 (12·50)	4 × 6,500 shp Soloviev TS	231,500 (105,000)	161 (260)	88
130	Aerospatiale/Westland SA 330E Puma	Medium transport helicopter	*49–2½ (15·00)	59–6½ (18·15)	16–10½ (5·14)	2 × 1,185 shp Turboméca Turmo TS	14,770 (6,700)	169 (272)	88
131	Fairey Rotodyne	VTOL transport prototype	*104–0 (31·72)	64–6 (19·67)	23–2 (7·06)	2 × 3,000 shp Napier Eland TP	33,000 (14,980)	191 (307)	90
132	Bell X–1	Supersonic research aircraft	28–0 (8·54)	31–0 (9·45)	10–10 (3·30)	1 × 6,000 lb st Reaction Motors RE	13,400** (6,354)	Mach 1·0 +	91
133	Bell X–2	Supersonic research aircraft	32–0 (9·75)	44–0 (13·41)	13–6 (4·11)	1 Curtiss XLR–25 of 15,000 lb st RE	——	2,148 (3,457)	91
134	Bell X–5	Variable-geometry research aircraft	32–9 (9·98)	32–4 (9·85)	12–0 (3·66)	1 × 4,900 lb st Allison TJ	10,000 (4,540)	Mach 1·0 +	91
135	North American X–15–A2	Advanced supersonic research aircraft	22–0 (6·70)	52–5 (15·98)	——	1 × 57,000 lb st Thiokol RE	50,914** (23,095)	Mach 6·0 +	91
136	Hawker Siddeley P.1127 F(GA) Mk 1	V/STOL close-support and reconnaissance aircraft	22–11 (6·98)	42–6 (12·95)	10–9 (3·28)	1 × 15,200 Bristol Siddeley Pegasus TF	15,500 (7,030)	Mach 0·87	92
137	Hawker Siddeley Harrier GR. Mk 1	V/STOL close-support and reconnaissance aircraft	25–3 (7·70)	45–6 (13·87)	11–3 (3·43)	1 × 20,000 lb st Rolls-Royce Pegasus 102 TF	25,000 + (11,339) +	737 + (1,186) +	92
138	Canadair CL–84–1	Tilt-wing V/STOL research aircraft	33–4 (10·16)	47–3½ (14·41)	14–2¾ (4·34)	2 × 1,500 shp Lycoming TP	E 13,300 (6,033)	E 321 (517)	93
139	Boeing-Vertol Model 347	Research helicopter	NOT KNOWN					202 (325)	94
140	Lake LA–4	Four-seat amphibian	38–0 (11·58)	24–11 (7·60)	9–4 (2·84)	1 × 180 hp Lycoming RA	2,400 (1,089)	135 (217)	94
141	Dornier Do 31 E	Experimental V/STOL transport aircraft	59–3 (18·06)	67–11 (20·70)	28–0 (8·53)	2 × 15,500 lb st TF 8 × 4,400 lb st TJ	60,600 (27,500)	400 (650)	95
142	Martin Marietta X–24B	Lifting-body research aircraft	†19–2 (5·84)	37–6 (11·43)	10–4 (3·15)	1 × 8,000 lb st Thiokol XLR–11 RE	13,000** (5,896)	E 1,000 (1,609)	95
143	LTV–Hiller–Ryan XC–142A	Experimental tilt-wing V/STOL transport	67–6 (20·57)	58–1 (17·71)	26–1 (7·95)	4 × 3,080 shp General Electric TP	44,500 (20,185)	409 (658)	96–97
144	North American Rockwell Quail Commander	Agricultural aircraft	34–9 (10·59)	23–6 (7·16)	7–7 (2·31)	1 × 290 hp Lycoming RA	3,600 (1,633)	120 (193)	98
145	Canadair CL–215	Multi-purpose amphibian	93–10 (28·60)	65–0¼ (19·82)	29–5½ (8·98)	2 × 2,100 hp Pratt & Whitney RA	43,500 (19,731)	172 (293)	99

NOTES: The information given in these tables applies specifically to the Mark or Series of machine quoted in the column headed aircraft. It does not necessarily apply to the particular aircraft illustrated as being representative of the type.

* An asterisk in the wing span column denotes a **rotary-wing aircraft.** Dimension quoted is that of the main rotor/s.

** Two asterisks in the max take-off weight column denotes that the aircraft is **air-launched.**

† This dimension, quoted under wing span, is the **maximum width** of this aircraft's lifting-body.

For **variable-geometry** aircraft the wing-span quoted is the maximum with wings unswept. Any figures preceded by the initial E are estimated.

Power plant. The number of engines is given as, for example, 4 ×, indicating four engines. The power output is quoted in horsepower for piston engines, shaft horsepower for turboprop and turboshaft engines, and in pounds static thrust for all other turbines and rocket engines. The two capital letters indicate the type of engine, using the following code: H: *horizontally opposed* I: *in-line* R: *radial* RE: *rocket-engine* TF: *turbofan* TJ: *turbojet* TP: *turboprop* TS: *turboshaft.* Terminating letter A denotes *air-cooled*; L, *liquid-cooled.*

Acknowledgments

The author and publishers are deeply indebted to those individuals and companies who have been kind enough to loan the colour transparencies that have made the illustrations of this book. Except as detailed by illustration number below, they come from the collection of *Mr. John W. R. Taylor.*

Air France 94
Air Portraits 1, 14, 29, 69, 141
The Boeing Company 37, 74, 75, 76, 77, 83, 84, 88, 117
British Aircraft Corporation 102, 111
Hawker Siddeley Aviation Ltd. 23, 97, 136, 137
Leslie Hunt 26, 57, 58, 59, 60, 61, 73, 80, 81
Howard Levy 2, 3, 4, 6, 15, 16, 49, 82
Lockheed Aircraft Corporation 100, 114
National Aeronautics and Space Administration 142, 146, 147, 148, 149
Northrop Corporation 51
Quantas Airways Ltd. 99
John Rigby Jacket, 11
Brian M. Service 101
Teledyne Ryan Aeronautical 21, 22
Westland Aircraft Ltd. 130